الاستنباط من البحر العميق

AL- ISTINBÃTU MIN AL BAHRI AL A'MÌQ

DROPS FROM THE DEEP OCEAN

REFLECTIONS ON THE QUR'AN

Human Valuation Systems, Social Constructs, Reductionism, and the Role of Scholars

with a focus on

- Contemporary Renderings
- Psychological Explorations
- Western Discourses
- Lexical Analysis

VOLUME 6

Dr. M. Yunus Kumek

Address to the Islamic Religious Scholars & Philosophers

Cover Photo by Y. Kumek, Alexandria, Egypt, January 12, 2019.

Medina House
publishing

www.medinahouse.org
170 Manhattan Ave, Po. Box 63
New York 14215
contact@medinahouse.org

ISBN 978-1-950979-33-2

Published in the United States of America.

TABLE OF CONTENTS

VOLUME 6

بِسْمِ اللهِ الرَّحْمَنِ الرَّحِيمِ[1]

الْحَمْدُ لِلَّهِ رَبِّ الْعَالَمِينَ[2]

اللَّهُمَّ صلِّ عَلى سَيِّدِناَ وَ حَبِيْبَنا وَ مَوْلَنَا مُحَمَّدٍ[3]

Preface

My Dear Friend,

Real friendship requires helping, sharing, and checking on each other. I find these treaties to be very helpful for my own ego and raw self. You can read with me. These treaties will help cure some of our spiritual and mental diseases and even inshAllah, cure our physical diseases. At these times, we need to renew our imãn constantly with the language that these diseases are presented. The remedy of each disease can be given by Allah ﷻ in its own means and language. InshAllah, we should keep ourselves in our dua, prayers, remembering each other and mentioning our names at least once a week. If we don't have the means to meet each other in this world physically, we will inshAllah meet in the akhirah. May Allah ﷻ grant us the shafa'ah of Rasulullah ﷺ and gather in Jannah with him ﷺ, Amìn!

What is the Qurãn

As one analyzes the Qurãn, one can realize three usûli principles or approaches. The first one is to review the meanings of a topic in a verse with its relation to the entire Qurãn and specifically with its relation to that specific surah. The second is to review the meanings of the same topic in accordance with the relation to the ayahs and sentences. The third is to review the meanings of the same topic in accordance with the relation of the selection of each word for that topic and the relation of the words with other words. Each word, conjunction, phrase, or small-looking term is selected very perfectly, systematically, and analytically.

1. In the name of Allah, the Entirely Merciful, the Especially Merciful.
2. [All] praise is [due] to Allah, Lord of the worlds.
3. O Allah, bless our master, our beloved, and Mawlana Muhammed (PBUH).

If one tries to think about a close alternative for a word, it is impossible to replace without the delivered meanings being lost within this word's relation with the ayah, with the surah and with other surahs in the entirety of the Qurãn.

VOLUME 6

Juz 1

Surah Fātiha

[1][4]

A Person of بِسْمِ اللّٰهِ

بِسْمِ اللّٰهِ الرَّحْمَنِ الرَّحِيمِ {الفاتحة/1}

The beginning of the Qurān with بِسْمِ اللّٰهِ shows us the foundation of Islam.

The foundation of Islām is tawhid. The phrase of بِسْمِ اللّٰهِ is the tawhid.

When a person views all of the world, the universe, personal and social encounters with بِسْمِ اللّٰهِ, then this person is called a mu'min. When a person views anything without بِسْمِ اللّٰهِ, then this person makes shirk with Allah ﷻ. He or she denies the Divine Mashiyyah, Allowance of Allah ﷻ.

A person of بِسْمِ اللّٰهِ has the courage. A person of بِسْمِ اللّٰهِ is not scared of anything except Allah ﷻ. When people are all panicking because of the disasters, evil-seeming disasters, the person of بِسْمِ اللّٰهِ smiles and knows that everything works with بِسْمِ اللّٰهِ. If Allah ﷻ does not allow or permit, not anything can come to existence even before they occur in our realms.

A person of بِسْمِ اللّٰهِ gets hikmah and wisdom from everything. A person of بِسْمِ اللّٰهِ learns from his or her mistakes. A person of بِسْمِ اللّٰهِ learns from an animal. A person of بِسْمِ اللّٰهِ learns from the plants. A person of بِسْمِ اللّٰهِ learns from physics, math, oceanology, and other sciences. All of this knowledge increases the yaqîn of the person of بِسْمِ اللّٰهِ. All of this knowledge for him or her has relevance, purpose, and meaning on the path of Allah ﷻ.

On the other hand, a person who is a lost wanderer is always in chaos. He or she does not know how to assign meanings with even simple things in life. A light breeze comes. He or she swings in one direction. Another breeze comes and she or he swings in another direction. A lost wanderer does not have a foundation. Therefore, he or she goes with the flow. A person who is like a lost wanderer ignores his or her spiritual self. He or she just considers the physical body as the self. She or he is always in fear, anxiety, and stress. If a disease comes, she

4. In the name of Allah ﷻ, the Entirely Merciful, the Especially Merciful.

panics. If something happens, he gets horrified. She or he lives a life of punishment in this world.

A true person of بِسْمِ الله lives a life of amazement and pleasure in this life. A true person of بِسْمِ الله is welcomed after death to the next of level of amazements and pleasures. She or he can feel as though they are in Part II of the same movie of amazing pleasure.

For the true person of, بِسْمِ الله Part I contains the pleasures and amazements in this world and Part II contains the pleasures and amazements of the next life after death as mentioned[5] قَالُواْ هَذَا الَّذِي رُزِقْنَا مِن قَبْلُ وَأُتُواْ بِهِ مُتَشَابِهاً وَلَهُمْ فِيهَا أَزْوَاجٌ مُّطَهَّرَةٌ وَهُمْ فِيهَا خَالِدُونَ {البقرة/25}.

Juz 2 & 3

Sûrah 2 – al-Baqara

[23-24][6]

وَإِن كُنتُمْ فِي رَيْبٍ مِّمَّا نَزَّلْنَا عَلَى عَبْدِنَا فَأْتُواْ بِسُورَةٍ مِّن مِّثْلِهِ وَادْعُواْ شُهَدَاءكُم مِّن دُونِ اللّهِ إِنْ كُنْتُمْ صَادِقِينَ {البقرة/23} فَإِن لَّمْ تَفْعَلُواْ وَلَن تَفْعَلُواْ فَاتَّقُواْ النَّارَ الَّتِي وَقُودُهَا النَّاسُ وَالْحِجَارَةُ أُعِدَّتْ لِلْكَافِرِينَ {البقرة/24}

One can analyze the preference of إن over the preference of اذا in the expression of وَإِن كُنتُمْ فِي رَيْبٍ. The word اذا can indicate the possibility of the occurrence of something. This word اذا can be translated in this context as the word 'when' in English. The word إن can indicate a hypothetical occurrence of something. The word إن can be translated as the word 'if' in English.

The presence of إن over اذا can indicate that their skepticism is all illusion, not grounded, and its basis is not existent in reality. One can translate this as "if you have it..." compared to "when you have it..."

5. And give good tidings to those who believe and do righteous deeds that they will have gardens [in Paradise] beneath which rivers flow. Whenever they are provided with a provision of fruit therefrom, they will say, "This is what we were provided with before." And it is given to them in likeness. And they will have therein purified spouses, and they will abide therein eternally.

6. 23. And if you are in doubt about what We have sent down (the Qurān) upon Our Servant Prophet Muúammad (s.a.w) then produce a s´rah the like thereof and call upon your witnesses supporters other than Allah ﷻ, if you should be truthful. 24. But if you do not—and you will never be able to—then fear the Fire, whose fuel is men and stones, prepared for the disbelievers.

At another perspective, the Qurãn is perfect, flawless, and complete. The discussions of skepticism and doubt are all human-related concepts or social constructs.

The word إِن can indicate that if there is any doubt, then it belongs to the addressee, the one who is spoken to. The concept or understanding of doubt does not exist for Allah ﷻ. The notion of doubt, skepticism, or uncertainty belongs to humans. The concept of doubt or skepticism is a human phenomenon.

The word إِن can also indicate that if there is a doubt, then these doubts can be removed. In other words, these doubts are not of any kind that they cannot be removed.

The phrase of كُنتُمْ in the expression وَإِن كُنتُمْ فِي رَيْبٍ can indicate their constant occupation with skepticism.

The word رَيْبٍ is in tanwin, nakrah form. This can indicate a lot of doubts of different kinds.

The word, harf-jar فِي in فِي رَيْبٍ can indicate the depth of this skepticism. In other words, فِي with فِي رَيْبٍ can indicate an embodiment of negative skepticism. The further stages of negative skepticism can sometimes cause the person to disconnect from the reality and can lead to schizophrenia. The definition of this disease is [1]:

> a long-term mental disorder of a type involving a breakdown in the relation between thought, emotion, and behavior, leading to faulty perception, inappropriate actions and feelings, withdrawal from reality and personal relationships into fantasy and delusion, and a sense of mental fragmentation.

In this sense, one calls or refers to positive skepticism as critical thinking to differentiate right from wrong, falsehood from truth and reality. A person in this sense should use all of his or her faculties to engage themselves with critical thinking in all parts of their life. Any type of informational, emotional, and physical abuse that is displayed in individuals is due to the lack of a sound critical thinking mechanism in the person.

The expression مِّمَّا نَزَّلْنَا with the combination of من and ما in مِّمَّا can indicate a piece as indicated in the balagah of the Qurãn. In other words, the Qurãn challenges the people to bring even a piece to prove their case similar to the ones in the Qurãn. The word بِسُورَةٍ itself can also indicate this challenge if they want to bring a piece such as one chapter, sûrah of the Qurãn.

One can view, in this example, this balãgah of the Qurãn through the piece approach in the other phrases or words. The form of نَزَّلْنَا can indicate also a piece-by-piece revelation of the Qurãn in 23 years. This again indicates the piece approach to support the previous words in the same ayah indicating the same meanings. One can remember that the form , أنزَلْنَاهُ for example in[7], {الدخان/3} إِنَّا أَنزَلْنَاهُ فِي لَيْلَةٍ مُّبَارَكَةٍ إِنَّا كُنَّا مُنذِرِينَ or[8] {القدر/1} إِنَّا أَنزَلْنَاهُ فِي لَيْلَةِ الْقَدْرِ can indicate the revelation of the entire Qurãn but not the piece-by-piece inzãl, revelation.

This is all balãgah of the Qurãn. Every word individually supports and indicate the entire message. In other words, one can find the entire message or meaning in a single word in the Qurãn.

When we analyze the expression[9] ,وَإِن كُنتُمْ فِي رَيْبٍ مِّمَّا نَزَّلْنَا عَلَى عَبْدِنَا the word, harfi-Jar عَلَى can indicate:

- The noble and high position of the revelation, wahiyy
- The given responsibility of the revelation and messengership on the Prophet ﷺ
- The heavy and serious responsibility of this duty of messengership.

The word عَبْدِنَا can indicate the most important quality of the Prophet ﷺ is being a'bd of Allah ﷻ. The highest rank of Rasulullah ﷺ is due to his ﷺ 'ubudiyyah to Allah ﷻ.

He has been elevated with mirãj with u'budiyyah as mentioned:[10] سُبْحَانَ الَّذِي أَسْرَى بِعَبْدِهِ لَيْلاً مِّنَ الْمَسْجِدِ الْحَرَامِ إِلَى الْمَسْجِدِ الأَقْصَى الَّذِي بَارَكْنَا حَوْلَهُ لِنُرِيَهُ مِنْ آيَاتِنَا إِنَّهُ هُوَ السَّمِيعُ الْبَصِيرُ {الإسراء/1}. In this case, one of the most important qualities of Rasulullah ﷺ is presented with the word عَبْدِنَاin the ayah.

The pronoun نَا in the word عَبْدِنَا can indicate the special, unique position of Rasulullah ﷺ in this ubudiyyah of Allah ﷻ.

7. Indeed, We sent the Qur'an down during the Night of Decree.
8. Indeed, We sent it down during a blessed night. Indeed, We were to warn [mankind].
9. And if you are in doubt about what We have sent down upon Our Servant [Muhammad ﷺ]
10. Exalted is He who took His Servant [i.e., Prophet Muhammad ﷺ by night from al-Masjid al-Haram to al-Masjid al-Aqsa whose surroundings We have blessed, to show him of Our signs. Indeed, He is the Hearing, the Seeing.

As the expression[11] عَلَى عَبْدِنَا can indicate the high status of Rasulullah ﷺ, this can indicate the high status of the hadith and sunnah of Rasulullah ﷺ. There is the classification of the recited revelation as wahy-I matluw, and the unrecited revelation as gayri-matluw. Wahy-matluw is the Qurãn. Gayri-matluw is the sunnah and hadith of Rasulullah ﷺ. The expression عَلَى عَبْدِنَا can indicate both types of revelations. Allahu'A'lam.

When we review the expression[12] فَأْتُوا بِسُورَةٍ مِّن مِّثْلِهِ, the word فَأْتُوا can indicate something for them to bring. Yet, in this struggle of looking into bringing something similar to a sûrah of the Qurãn, it is hoped that they can understand the value of the Qurãn and have imãn and guidance.

When we analyze the word بِسُورَةٍ in فَأْتُوا بِسُورَةٍ, this word سُورَةٍ and سور have similar root words. In this regard, 'sûrah', each chapter of the Qurãn is similar to a 'sûr', a protected castle. In the context of this ãyah, it is impossible to challenge the Qurãn and even a sûrah of the Qurãn. Each sûrah of the Qurãn is like a protected castle.

When we analyze the expression مِّن مِّثْلِهِ, this can indicate that the opposing group can present some arguments and documents in their deception in their struggle to confront the Qurãn. Yet, the expression مِّن مِّثْلِهِ can indicate that what they may possibly bring is not similar to the Qurãn. The source of the Qurãn is not from an ummi nabiyy ﷺ. Yet, he ﷺ only delivers the message to others that is revealed to him ﷺ. This is mentioned in many places in the Qurãn as:[13] قُلْ إِنَّمَا أَنَا بَشَرٌ مِّثْلُكُمْ يُوحَىٰ إِلَيَّ أَنَّمَا إِلَٰهُكُمْ إِلَٰهٌ وَاحِدٌ فَمَن كَانَ يَرْجُو لِقَاءَ رَبِّهِ فَلْيَعْمَلْ عَمَلًا صَالِحًا وَلَا يُشْرِكْ بِعِبَادَةِ رَبِّهِ أَحَدًا {الكهف/110}

قُلْ إِنَّمَا يُوحَىٰ إِلَيَّ أَنَّمَا إِلَٰهُكُمْ إِلَٰهٌ وَاحِدٌ فَهَلْ أَنتُم مُّسْلِمُونَ {الأنبياء/108} [14]

إِن يُوحَىٰ إِلَيَّ إِلَّا أَنَّمَا أَنَا نَذِيرٌ مُّبِينٌ {ص/70} [15]

The expression of يُوحَىٰ إِلَيَّ explicitly declares the position of Rasulullah ﷺ and the position of all the prior anbiyã, the prophets and messengers

11. upon Our Servant [Muhammad ﷺ]
12. then produce a surah the like thereof
13. Say, "I am only a man like you, to whom has been revealed that your god is one God. So whoever would hope for the meeting with his Lord – let him do righteous work and not associate in the worship of his Lord anyone."
14. He will say, "Remain despised therein and do not speak to Me.
15. It has not been revealed to me except that I am a clear warner.

of Allah ﷻ. They are only messengers who are relating a message from Rabbul A'lamìn, Allah ﷻ.

When we analyze the expression, إِنْ كُنْتُمْ صَادِقِينَ[16] one can remember the original discussions about their statements such as, "We can bring a book like Muhammad did." Astagfirullah, this statement or similar ones were some of the early Meccans' responses when Rasulullah ﷺ was reciting the noble ayahs of the Qurãn to the people of that society.

One can view the implicit hasad, jealousy, and envy in the above type statement which is hidden in the expression إِنْ كُنْتُمْ صَادِقِينَ. The above statement or disposition triggers the person's internal emotions regardless of the reality and truthfulness. They are not aware of their own selves nor have they much awareness about what they are saying or claiming. In this regard, the expression إِنْ كُنْتُمْ صَادِقِينَ is a reminder to bring them into their real states of self and away from the agitated states of envy, jealousy, or hasad. In other words, some people run from the realities and the truth on the donkey of hasad, jealousy with loud, ugly internal screaming without making much progress.

May Allah ﷻ protect us from involving ourselves in hasad and jealousy when we face or are presented with realities, Amìn!

Taqwa due to Mercy

As there many definitions of taqwa as mentioned فَاتَّقُواْ, one of the possible meanings that can be reflected in the translation of this word is to seek refuge in Allah ﷻ. In other words, taqwa is the act of running to Allah ﷻ for protection and taking shelter in Allah ﷻ. Taqwa is not mere avoidance or abstinence as is classically translated as 'being afraid of Allah ﷻ and therefore avoiding something'. Yet, this word can indicate the purposeful and active effort of a person running to Allah ﷻ for protection and taking refuge.

In this sense, the word اجتنبوا is not used. The word اجتنبوا can indicate mere avoidance, and keeping oneself distanced from an undesired situation. Instead, the word فَاتَّقُوا is used. This word designates avoidance by taking shelter and seeking protection in Allah ﷻ.

Therefore, even the expression فَاتَّقُواْ النَّارَ can signify the Rahmah, Mercy of Allah ﷻ. The expression فَاتَّقُواْ النَّارَ with the word فَاتَّقُوا can

16. If you should be truthful.

suggest running to Allah ﷻ to take shelter and find protection in Allah ﷻ.

This can be similar to a child's relationship with the mother. When there is a harm, the mother warns the child about this harm. Then the child run backs to mother and hugs her tightly in order to take shelter and find protection in her.

The Mercy of Allah ﷻ on a person is much stronger than a mother has for her child as mentioned by Rasulullah ﷺ [2] (5653). The word taqwa in that sense emphasizes running back to Mercy, Protection, and Caring of Allah ﷻ from all the harms.

Calling for Help

When we analyze the expression وَادْعُوا شُهَدَاءكُم مِّن دُونِ اللّهِ, the word وَادْعُوا can indicate their helplessness, panic, and anxiety. This word وَادْعُوا can also indicate a scene of a person or people shouting for help with panic. It is interesting to note that in all cases of their position with the Qurãn the same word وَادْعُوا is used as:[17]

أَمْ يَقُولُونَ افْتَرَاهُ قُلْ فَأْتُواْ بِسُورَةٍ مِّثْلِهِ وَادْعُواْ مَنِ اسْتَطَعْتُم مِّن دُونِ اللّهِ إِن كُنتُمْ صَادِقِينَ {يونس/38}

أَمْ يَقُولُونَ افْتَرَاهُ قُلْ فَأْتُواْ بِعَشْرِ سُوَرٍ مِّثْلِهِ مُفْتَرَيَاتٍ وَادْعُواْ مَنِ اسْتَطَعْتُم مِّن دُونِ[18] اللّهِ إِن كُنتُمْ صَادِقِينَ {هود/13}

One can especially realize the case of panic, anxiety, and a shouting scene in the ayah as[19] قُلِ ادْعُواْ الَّذِينَ زَعَمْتُم مِّن دُونِهِ فَلاَ يَمْلِكُونَ كَشْفَ الضُّرِّ عَنكُمْ وَلاَ تَحْوِيلاً {الإسراء/56}. When a person is in harm's way as mentioned الضُّرِّ, the person is expected to shout, call, and invite others to help as the word ادْعُوا can indicate.

This word has an especially negative meaning when it is used for something other than Allah ﷻ. One can see this in

17. Or do they say [about the Prophet (s.a.w)], "He invented it?" Say, "Then bring forth a surah like it and call upon [for assistance] whomever you can besides Allah ﷻ, if you should be truthful."

18. Or do they say, "He invented it"? Say, "Then bring ten s´rahs like it that have been invented and call upon [for assistance] whomever you can besides Allah ﷻ if you should be truthful."

19. And cause not corruption upon the earth after its reformation. And invoke Him in fear and aspiration. Indeed, the mercy of Allah ﷻ is near to the doers of good.

{الأعراف/194} إِنَّ الَّذِينَ تَدْعُونَ مِن دُونِ اللَّهِ عِبَادٌ أَمْثَالُكُمْ فَادْعُوهُمْ فَلْيَسْتَجِيبُوا [20] لَكُمْ إِن كُنتُمْ صَادِقِينَ

أَلَهُمْ أَرْجُلٌ يَمْشُونَ بِهَا أَمْ لَهُمْ أَيْدٍ يَبْطِشُونَ بِهَا أَمْ لَهُمْ أَعْيُنٌ يُبْصِرُونَ بِهَا أَمْ لَهُمْ آذَانٌ [21] يَسْمَعُونَ بِهَا قُلِ ادْعُوا شُرَكَاءَكُمْ ثُمَّ كِيدُونِ فَلَا تُنظِرُونِ {الأعراف/195}

It is very scary that the people who are panicking and calling to others in this life- other than Allah ﷻ as mentioned with this word -,وَادْعُوا they are now encouraged to call in vain with panic with this word وَادْعُوا in the akhirah as: [22] قَالُوا أَوَلَمْ تَكُ تَأْتِيكُمْ رُسُلُكُم بِالْبَيِّنَاتِ قَالُوا بَلَىٰ قَالُوا فَادْعُوا وَمَا دُعَاءُ الْكَافِرِينَ إِلَّا فِي ضَلَالٍ {غافر/50}

This is the position of humiliation. May Allah ﷻ protect us, Amìn.

One should remember who to call, who to really panic from, and who to take refuge in, and who to expect any results from. The only One, but the only, is Allah .ﷻ In this regard, this word وَادْعُوا only goes back to, in its real and absolute usage, for Allah .ﷻ This is mentioned as:[23]

وَقَالَ رَبُّكُمُ ادْعُونِي أَسْتَجِبْ لَكُمْ إِنَّ الَّذِينَ يَسْتَكْبِرُونَ عَنْ عِبَادَتِي سَيَدْخُلُونَ جَهَنَّمَ دَاخِرِينَ {غافر/60}

In this regard, Allah ﷻ specifies the usage of this word وَادْعُوا only for the Divine Zãt, Allah ﷻ, as mentioned ادْعُونِي. This is specified with the pronoun ي in ادْعُونِي, SubhanAllah! Therefore, all the fruitful results of calls, dua, any help or outcome are only from Allah ﷻ. This is underlined and explicitly stated in أَسْتَجِبْ لَكُمْ with the mutakalllim prounoun in أَسْتَجِبْ.

In other words, when the person truly, sincerely, and directly calls Allah ﷻ without any shirk, Allah ﷻ answers these calls. Yet, when the person includes implicit or explicit shirk in this calling, although the

---

20. Indeed, those you [polytheists] call upon besides Allah ﷻ are servants [i.e., creations] like you. So call upon them and let them respond to you,if you should be truthful.
21. Do they have feet by which they walk? Or do they have hands by which they strike? Or do they have eyes by which they see? Or do they have ears by which they hear? Say, [O Muhammad ﷺ],"Call your 'partners' and then conspire against me and give me no respite.
22. [They will be told],"That is because, when Allah ﷻ was called upon alone, you disbelieved; but if others were associated with Him, you believed. So the judgment is with Allah ﷻ, the Most High, the Grand."
23. And your Lord says,"Call upon Me; I will respond to you." Indeed, those who disdain My worship will enter Hell [rendered] contemptible.

person may think that he or she is calling Allah ﷻ, then the call may not be answered. May Allah ﷻ protect us.

Therefore, sincere dua and sincere call is only made to Allah ﷻ. Therefore, sincere worship or ibadah is only made for Allah ﷻ. This is mentioned as عِبَادَتِي with, again, the mutakallim pronoun of the Zãt of Allah ﷻ with ي.

The essence of ibadah is the dua. Both the external and internal should be for Allah ﷻ. The external is the ibadah for Allah SWT. The internal is the call, dua, to Allah ﷻ. May Allah ﷻ make us from the true and sincere callers of Allah ﷻ, Amìn.

When we analyze the expression, وَادْعُواْ شُهَدَاءكُم مِّن دُونِ اللّهِ the expression مِّن دُونِ اللّهِ can indicate any being other than Allah .ﷻ In this regard, this confrontation of the Qurãn can indicate anyone from humans, jinn, angels, or other any beings. Angels (alayhi salãm) will not have this type of absence of adab with the Kalãm of Allah .ﷻ Then, the only beings known to us that are left are humans and jinn. Therefore, in another ayah, Allah ﷻ mentions as the addressee of this challenge to be humans and jinn as قُل لَّئِنِ اجْتَمَعَتِ الإِنسُ وَالْجِنُّ عَلَى أَن يَأْتُواْ بِمِثْلِ هَذَا الْقُرْآنِ لاَ يَأْتُونَ بِمِثْلِهِ وَلَوْ كَانَ بَعْضُهُمْ لِبَعْضٍ ظَهِيرًا [24] {الإسراء/88}

Finite Element Analysis and the Qurãn

It is very interesting to analyze the interaction and the dynamics of the words in the expression فَإِن لَّمْ تَفْعَلُواْ وَلَن تَفْعَلُو. The word تَفْعَلُواْ is a verb of mudari. This verb has implications between the present and the future. The word إِن is a harf and indicates condition, shart. In this case, إِن implies a future time. The harf لَن can indicate the impossibility in the future.

On the other hand, the word لَّمْ is a harf that implies the past. In this case, the word or the verb تَفْعَلُواْ is similar to a bouncing ball between the past, present, and future.

In its totality, this can show that it is impossible to challenge or confront the Qurãn. In the past, it was not possible. Nor today, is it possible. Also, it will not be possible in the future.

24. Say, "If mankind and the jinn gathered in order to produce the like of this Quran, they could not produce the like of it, even if they were to each other assistants."

This is again another ijãz of the Qurãn—that it gives the entirety of the meaning in a small expression of[25] فَإِن لَّمْ تَفْعَلُوا وَلَن تَفْعَلُو.

This style of the Qurãn is not unique to only this ayah. One can observe this intended totality of the meanings of the ayah or sûrah in words or individual expressions.

One can refer to this as finite element analysis (FEA)in mathematical modeling of the perspectives of the Qurãn.

In that sense, if a classical linguist approaches the Qurãn, that person may approach this by making a general term of balagah to show the I'jaz of the Qurãn.

Yet, a mathematician, civil engineer, or a computer engineer can express the same phenomenon within their field of expertise.

In this case, if one takes an ayah of the Qurãn, one can realize the overall intended meaning of the ayah in the individual words and expressions of the same ayah. In this case, it is important to focus on the below definition of FEA.

Finite Element Analysis or FEA is the simulation of a physical phenomenon using a numerical mathematic technique referred to as the Finite Element Method, or FEM. This process is at the core of mechanical engineering, as well as a variety of other disciplines. It also is one of the key principles used in the development of simulation software. Engineers can use these FEM to reduce the number of physical prototypes and run virtual experiments to optimize their designs. To run an FEA simulation, a mesh is first generated, containing millions of small elements that make up the overall shape. This is a way of transcribing a 3D object into a series of mathematical points that can then be analyzed. The density of this mesh can be altered based upon how complex or simple a simulation is needed. Calculations are run for every single element or point of the mesh and then combined to make up the overall final result for the structure. Since the calculations are done on a mesh, rather than the entirety of a physical object, it means that some interpolation needs to occur between the points. These approximations are usually within the bounds of what's needed. The points of the mesh where the data is known mathematically are referred to as nodal points and tend to be grouped around boundaries or other areas of change in an object's design [1].

---

25. But if you do not—and you will never be able to

With the above definition of FEA, what we are really doing is interpolation of very obvious points. Yet, the people who don't know how to make interpolation may not get a meaning or meanings from the overall intended meanings of the Qurãn. Here, the term mesh is used for taking a sample of expression and analyzing it through and with the overall structure. If people are amazed and believe that today's advanced technology is realized and achieved with FEA, the amazements of the Qurãn by using the FEA can mean much more than other ones, Allahu A'lam.

Impossibility of Production of a Challenge & Miracles of the Qurãn

One can ask about the expression[26] فَإِن لَّمْ تَفْعَلُواْ وَلَن تفعلوا, why instead of the verb تَفْعَلُوا another verb such as تاتوا can be used. Why is there the preference of the تَفْعَلُوا ?

One can realize that if the verb تاتوا was used, this would imply an indication that the Qurãn can be challenged, but they don't know how to challenge the Qurãn. In other words, the problem is them.

Yet, the word تَفْعَلُواْ is used in order to underline that the problem of possibility of challenge is not related to who 'they' are. There is no one who has the ability and capacity of making anything similar to the Qurãn as the verb تَفْعَلُواْ can indicate.

In this regard, تَفْعَلُواْ can indicate making and تاتوا can indicate presenting their arguments. Yet, they are incapacitated at the level of the production of their arguments before they even present them, SubhanAllah!

This is another Ij'ã z of the Qurãn.

There is another possible indication of the verb choice of تَفْعَلُواْ. As one may know, the three letters, ف، ع، ل are the measuring stick of all actions as used in Arabic morphology. In this regard, this can indicate all of humans' possible actions to challenge the Qurãn. Yet this word, including its morphological usage, can indicate all other verbs' actions with their impossibilities.

26. But if you do not—and you will never be able to

This is another Ij'ã z of the Qurãn.

The expression [27] فَاتَّقُوا النَّارَ has the preference of the word 'ittiqa' instead of other words such as 'ijtinãb'. The preference of the word 'ittiqa' can imply imãn due to its link with taqwa. A word such as 'ijtinãb' may not remind the person of the link of the word with necessity to imãn. In other words, the usage of the فَاتَّقُوا can imply that if you want to be protected from the punishment of fire, then have imãn which necessitates taqwa.

This is another Ij'ã z of the Qurãn.

The expression of[28] وَقُودُهَا النَّاسُ وَالْحِجَارَةُ can indicate burning rocks such as coal. Coal is defined as a combustible black or dark brown rock consisting mainly of carbonized plant matter, found mainly in underground deposits and widely used as fuel [2].

This can indicate different metallurgic related discoveries that have value for humans. The value can be related to their property of combustibility such as coal or other properties that humans can use in different applications, Allahu A'lam.

One can also review the definition of petroleum as a liquid mixture of hydrocarbons that is present in certain rock strata and can be extracted and refined to produce fuels including gasoline, kerosene, and diesel oil; oil [2].

They all have relation with rocks in their combustibility as the ayah indicates with[29] الْحِجَارَةُ.

From the prospective initial interpretations of this ayah by our salãf, the word الْحِجَارَةُ can indicate the idols of early people before Islãm, worshipping them in their material forms such as rocks or stones [3]. From this perspective, both the worshippers and worshipped items such as stones or rocks are in fire, punishment. May Allah ﷻ protect us.

This is another Ij'ãz of the Qurãn. Above are a few Ij'ãz of the Qurãn in one single ayah. In the ayah, the Ij'ãz is a small expression. In a small expression, there is the Ij'ãz in each word. SubhanAllah! One can realize these convoluted perspectives of Ij'ãz in all of the ayahs of the Qurãn collectively, individually, separately, and in grouping perspectives of surahs or maqta[30].

---

27. Then fear the Fire
28. Whose fuel is men and stones
29. Stones
30. Maqta is another term defined by the scholars of the field of Tafsìr to separate the beginning and ending of a new topic in the Qurãn.

رَيْبٍ —Rayb

When we analyze this ayah around the word[31] ,رَيْبٍ one can also realize that the same word is used in the beginning of the sûrah as [32] ذَٰلِكَ الْكِتَابُ لَا رَيْبَ فِيهِ هُدًى لِّلْمُتَّقِينَ {البقرة/2}. One can then ask: Why is this word رَيْبٍ emphasized with repetition after approximately twenty ayahs?

This can indicate a few points.

First, humans can approach the new teachings with رَيْبٍ. Historically, people have approached the scriptures and messengers regarding their authenticity with رَيْبٍ.

In today's time, one can consider this word as questioning leading to critical thinking on a positive note. From this perspective, it can be an attitude of humbleness, open-mindedness, and acceptance after this critical thinking process.

In another perspective, when the person knows and rationalizes the teachings of the Qurân and Rasulullah ﷺ, then some will still keep their strong identities as a hindrance and continue to be narrow-minded and intolerant. Strong club identities hinder their acceptance.

The Qurân suggests that the people with رَيْبٍ can bring a similar book to prove their stance. In that sense, فَأْتُوا can indicate something already prepared and worked on. In other words, bringing a book requires preparation. The Qurân asks them to bring one if there already is one.

Then, فَأْتُوا بِسُورَةٍ مِّن مِّثْلِهِ changes this premise and reduces it to levels to help them prove their stance. The first one is بِسُورَةٍ, not the entire book. The second one is مِّن مِّثْلِهِ, not the exact one but a comparable one. All of these need preparation, focus, analysis, and compilation on the part of the one who has رَيْبٍ to prove the opposing stance. In other words, the Qurân indicates that if you really want to bring something similar to the Qurân, then work on it diligently.

Yet, when someone is not successful in this type of diligent working, he or she may assume that there can be others who can achieve this task? Then, the Qurân opens the floor and encourages them to find the people who have the ability and strength as mentioned وَادْعُوا شُهَدَاءَكُم.

31. Doubt
32. This is the Book about which there is no doubt, a guidance for those conscious of Allah ﷻ

Yet, if the person cannot do it as mentioned فَإِن لَّمْ تَفْعَلُواْ, then the reason and logic require us to accept the pearl and diamond teachings of the Qurãn and eliminate this ungrounded رَيْبٍ.

Yet another very strong part ends this discussion with, "Know that no one can and will be able to justify their رَيْبٍ as mentioned وَلَن تَفْعَلُواْ!"

After all this, "Know that the fear of the accountability for your evil, unreasonable, and absurd stance should make you re-think and re-consider your oppressive stance as mentioned[33] فَاتَّقُواْ النَّارَ الَّتِي وَقُودُهَا النَّاسُ وَالْحِجَارَةُ أُعِدَّتْ لِلْكَافِرِينَ!" All the false stances are oppressions at different levels.

One can realize that the prophets had different miracles to prove their authenticity that Allah ﷻ had sent them. The Qurãn is the miracle of Rasulullah ﷺ. This miracle still exists and will exist with us until the End of Days. The Qurãn as a miracle proves both the authenticity of Rasulullah ﷺ and at the same time, the Qurãn delivers the message of Rabbul Alamìn to us.

Challenge of the Qurãn and the Wars

When one reviews the portion of the ayah as فَأْتُواْ بِسُورَةٍ, this is another miracle of the Qurãn. The shortest sûrah in the Qurãn is Sûrah al-Kawthar. The word بِسُورَةٍ with its form of diminutive- nakra can imply that this sûrah is the shortest sûrah in the Qurãn. In this regard, one can remember one of the only or one of the few attempts such as the embarrassing attempt of Musaylamatul Kazzãb of trying to use this sûrah and to change the wordings to try to make a challenge. Yet, he became humiliated by the Arab's who were at the highest level of expertise in the language and literature at the time. After this humiliation, there has been no cited or credible reported attempts in history.

One should remember that responding to the challenge of the Qurãn by bringing a similar text is an easier way for the people to challenge Islãm or Muslims as compared to the physical challenges of physical attacks or declaring wars against them. Especially, if one considers early Arabs at the time of Rasulullah ﷺ, they had the utmost expertise in language to challenge with another text if that had been possible.

33. then fear the Fire, whose fuel is men and stones, prepared for the disbelievers.

Yet, since this was impossible they sought solutions to challenge and pressure the early Muslims by physical force, attacks, and declared wars against them instead of the intellectual force of mind, writing, and critical thinking. Later, as this was impossible for Musaylamatul Kazzab as well, war against the sahabah was the same display of showing their weakness, powerlessness, and humiliation in front of the Qurãn. Throughout history and until today, because any challenge against the Qurãn has been impossible, people from the West or the East- or wherever the direction is representing this humility, embarrassment, and disablement against the Qurãn- tried to seek physical means of attack, violence, or wars against the Muslims.

In its reality, the issue is not really the Muslims. Their issue has been with the Qurãn as mentioned [34] قَدْ نَعْلَمُ إِنَّهُ لَيَحْزُنُكَ الَّذِي يَقُولُونَ فَإِنَّهُمْ لاَ يُكَذِّبُونَكَ وَلَكِنَّ الظَّالِمِينَ بِآيَاتِ اللّهِ يَجْحَدُونَ {الأنعام/33}. Their representation of disablement, bewilderment, and embarrassment against the Qurãn has been displayed in different forms of violence and attack.

When there is a truth from Rabbul Alamìn, such as the Qurãn, this can either give guidance and increase the person's imãn. Or, it can increase their embarrassment and humiliation, if they don't accept these teachings. Their dalalah, misguidance can be multiplied and increased as mentioned: [35] إِنَّ اللَّهَ لاَ يَسْتَحْيِي أَن يَضْرِبَ مَثَلاً مَّا بَعُوضَةً فَمَا فَوْقَهَا فَأَمَّا الَّذِينَ آمَنُواْ فَيَعْلَمُونَ أَنَّهُ الْحَقُّ مِن رَّبِّهِمْ وَأَمَّا الَّذِينَ كَفَرُواْ فَيَقُولُونَ مَاذَا أَرَادَ اللَّهُ بِهَذَا مَثَلاً يُضِلُّ بِهِ كَثِيراً وَيَهْدِي بِهِ كَثِيراً وَمَا يُضِلُّ بِهِ إِلاَّ الْفَاسِقِينَ {البقرة/26}.

In this regard, due to this anger of disablement against these genuine, true, pearl and diamond teachings of the Qurãn, they prefer to follow a sidetrack of attacking the ones, Muslims who accept the truth of the Qurãn.

In this regard, the story is the same. It is the jealousy, hasad, and group identities of selfishness. This concept is always like this: "If I don't have it or if I don't accept it, then you should not have it or accept it." Here is the source of the real disease. One can analyze this disease around the self and group-related identities.

---

34. We know that you, [O Muhammad ﷺ], are saddened by what they say. And indeed, they do not call you untruthful, but it is the verses of Allah that the wrongdoers reject.

35. Indeed, Allah ﷻ is not timid to present an example – that of a mosquito or what is smaller15 than it. And those who have believed know that it is the truth from their Lord. But as for those who disbelieve, they say, "What did Allah intend by this as an example?" He misleads many thereby and guides many thereby. And He misleads not except the defiantly disobedient,

Here is an example of this disease of hasad at an individual self-level as mentioned:[36]

وَاتْلُ عَلَيْهِمْ نَبَأَ ابْنَيْ آدَمَ بِالْحَقِّ إِذْ قَرَّبَا قُرْبَانًا فَتُقُبِّلَ مِن أَحَدِهِمَا وَلَمْ يُتَقَبَّلْ مِنَ الآخَرِ
قَالَ لَأَقْتُلَنَّكَ قَالَ إِنَّمَا يَتَقَبَّلُ اللّهُ مِنَ الْمُتَّقِينَ {المائدة/27} ئِن بَسَطتَ إِلَيَّ يَدَكَ لِتَقْتُلَنِي مَا
أَنَاْ بِبَاسِطٍ يَدِيَ إِلَيْكَ لَأَقْتُلَكَ إِنِّي أَخَافُ اللّهَ رَبَّ الْعَالَمِينَ {المائدة/28} إِنِّي أُرِيدُ أَن تَبُوءَ
بِإِثْمِي وَإِثْمِكَ فَتَكُونَ مِنْ أَصْحَابِ النَّارِ وَذَلِكَ جَزَاء الظَّالِمِينَ {المائدة/29} فَطَوَّعَتْ لَهُ
نَفْسُهُ قَتْلَ أَخِيهِ فَقَتَلَهُ فَأَصْبَحَ مِنَ الْخَاسِرِينَ{المائدة/30}

Here is an example of this disease of hasad at a group level as mentioned:[37]

قُلْ يَا أَهْلَ الْكِتَابِ هَلْ تَنقِمُونَ مِنَّا إِلاَّ أَنْ آمَنَّا بِاللّهِ وَمَا أُنزِلَ إِلَيْنَا وَمَا أُنزِلَ مِن قَبْلُ وَأَنَّ
أَكْثَرَكُمْ فَاسِقُونَ {المائدة/59}

The Purpose of Jahannam

On another note, the expression أُعِدَّتْ لِلْكَافِرِينَ can indicate the purpose of Jahannam. Although there are canonized approaches that a believer of Allah ﷻ can end up in Jahannam, May Allah ﷻ protect us, this ayah can indicate that the purpose of the existence of Jahannam is for the kuffār, but not for the believers. In other words, everything can have a primary purpose and goal. Yet, secondary effects do not replace this primary purpose.

Allah SWT has created the earth and skies for humans and jinn for a primary purpose and goal. Yet, there are other creation of Allah SWT such as animals and others who receive benefits from the secondary effects.

Similarly, in an institution such as a hospital, the primary people that can be running the show are doctors. Yet, there are other medical

---

36. 27. And recite to them the story of Adam's two sons, in truth, when they both offered a sacrifice [to Allah ﷻ], and it was accepted from one of them but was not accepted from the other. Said [the latter], "I will surely kill you." Said [the former], "Indeed, Allah ﷻ only accepts from the righteous [who fear Him]. 28. If you should raise your hand against me to kill me—I shall not raise my hand against you to kill you. Indeed, I fear Allah ﷻ, Lord of the worlds. 29. Indeed I want you to obtain [thereby] my sin and your sin so you will be among the companions of the Fire. And that is the recompense of wrongdoers." 30. And his soul permitted to him the murder of his brother, so he killed him and became among the losers.
37. Say, "O People of the Scripture, do you resent us except [for the fact] that we have believed in Allah ﷻ and what was revealed to us and what was revealed before and because most of you are defiantly disobedient?"

personnel who help and support the doctors in their work. In a university, the primary people that can be running the show are professors. Yet, there are other support staff to help them make the teaching possible.

In this case, the case of some of the believers being punished in Jahannam temporarily can be one of these secondary effects. To prove and establish this point, the shafa'ah of Rasulullah ﷺ as mentioned in the authentic sources of hadith [4] for every one holding even a tiny bit of imãn, even if it is smaller than a mustard seed, can also support this perspective.

In other words, in the Divine Mashiyyah of Allah ,ﷻ the existence of Jahannam is not for the believers as mentioned [38] أُعِدَّتْ لِلْكَافِرِينَ. Its existence is for the kuffãr. Rasulullah ﷺ has this Noble and High status to execute and display this Mashiyyah of Allah ﷻ in this world and in the afterlife.

In other words, Rasulullah ﷺ is given by Allah ﷻ this high status of being Rahmatun lil Alamìn as mentionedوَمَا أَرْسَلْنَاكَ إِلَّا رَحْمَةً لِّلْعَالَمِينَ [39] وَمَا أَرْسَلْنَاكَ إِلَّا كَافَّةً لِّلنَّاسِ بَشِيرًا وَنَذِيرًا وَلَٰكِنَّ أَكْثَرَ النَّاسِ لَا يَعْلَمُونَ {الأنبياء/107} and[40] {سبأ/28}.

Rasulullah ﷺ was sent for rahmah in this world and in the afterlife. He ﷺ completes his ﷺ mission and purpose with the famous and critical incident of Shaf'ah in the afterlife for everyone who has imãn [4].

In this case, this again indicates what the primary purpose of Jahannam is with the Mashiyyah of Allah ﷻas mentioned[41] أُعِدَّتْ لِلْكَافِرِينَ .

Question: Why does Allah ﷻ prepare a punishment for the creation that Allah ﷻ has created?

Answer: One of the hikmahs can be that it is not really to punish the humans or jinn but to deter and stop their purposeful engagements of evil, oppression, and kufr by reminding them of the accountability and consequences of their actions. This can form positive fear in order to stop them from evil engagements. Although this may not be the highest level of motivation for doing things in one's relationship with Allah ﷻ, yet it still causes the people who are operating at a lower level of a spiritual path to reconsider their actions and choices in life.

---

38. Prepared for the disbelievers.
39. And We have not sent you, [O Muhammad], except as a mercy to the worlds.
40. And We have not sent you except comprehensively to mankind as a bringer of good tidings and a warner. But most of the people do not know.
41. prepared for the disbelievers.

In other words, the fear of accountability can stop the crimes executed towards people and in one's relationship with Allah ﷻ.

One can realize this critical hikmah with the word[42] أُعِدَّتْ.

If one reviews the Qurãn, another ayah that shows this notion of preparation for a physical attack with a similar word أُعِدَّتْ with its purpose of deterrence with the word تُرْهِبُونَ بِهِ as mentioned:[43]

وَأَعِدُّواْ لَهُم مَّا اسْتَطَعْتُم مِّن قُوَّةٍ وَمِن رِّبَاطِ الْخَيْلِ تُرْهِبُونَ بِهِ عَدْوَّ اللّهِ وَعَدُوَّكُمْ وَآخَرِينَ مِن دُونِهِمْ لاَ تَعْلَمُونَهُمُ اللّهُ يَعْلَمُهُمْ وَمَا تُنفِقُواْ مِن شَيْءٍ فِي سَبِيلِ اللّهِ يُوَفَّ إِلَيْكُمْ وَأَنتُمْ لاَ تُظْلَمُونَ {الأنفال/60}

In this case, the purpose or hikmah is تُرْهِبُونَ بِهِ. This hikmah is to instill the notion of deterrence for an action with its consequence.

If someone tries to bully another person, if he or she knows the consequences, they may stop doing it.

If someone tries to abuse another person, if he or she knows the consequences, they may stop doing it.

If a group plans to attack another group, if they know the consequences, they may stop doing it.

The notion of deterrence can reflect itself in governmental relationships as well. In other words, kings, sultans, or presidents of a country can have a policy of deterrence by establishing a ministry of defense by forming defense mechanisms to instill fear of deterrence if other countries desire to attack them.

42. Prepared

43. And prepare against them whatever you are able of power and of steeds of war419 by which you may terrify the enemy of Allah ﷻ and your enemy and others besides them whom you do not know [but] whom Allah ﷻ knows. And whatever you spend in the cause of Allah will be fully repaid to you, and you will not be wronged.

One of these cases is vividly viewed in the Qurãn as:[44]

قَالَتْ يَا أَيُّهَا المَلَأُ إِنِّي أُلْقِيَ إِلَيَّ كِتَابٌ كَرِيمٌ {النمل/29} إِنَّهُ مِن سُلَيْمَانَ وَإِنَّهُ بِسْمِ اللَّهِ الرَّحْمَنِ الرَّحِيمِ {النمل/30} أَلَّا تَعْلُوا عَلَيَّ وَأْتُونِي مُسْلِمِينَ {النمل/31} قَالَتْ يَا أَيُّهَا المَلَأُ أَفْتُونِي فِي أَمْرِي مَا كُنتُ قَاطِعَةً أَمْرًا حَتَّى تَشْهَدُونِ {النمل/32} قَالُوا نَحْنُ أُوْلُوا قُوَّةٍ وَأُولُوا بَأْسٍ شَدِيدٍ وَالْأَمْرُ إِلَيْكِ فَانظُرِي مَاذَا تَأْمُرِينَ {النمل/33} قَالَتْ إِنَّ الْمُلُوكَ إِذَا دَخَلُوا قَرْيَةً أَفْسَدُوهَا وَجَعَلُوا أَعِزَّةَ أَهْلِهَا أَذِلَّةً وَكَذَلِكَ يَفْعَلُونَ {النمل/34} وَإِنِّي مُرْسِلَةٌ إِلَيْهِم بِهَدِيَّةٍ فَنَاظِرَةٌ بِمَ يَرْجِعُ الْمُرْسَلُونَ {النمل/35}

فَلَمَّا جَاء سُلَيْمَانَ قَالَ أَتُمِدُّونَنِ بِمَالٍ فَمَا آتَانِيَ اللَّهُ خَيْرٌ مِّمَّا آتَاكُم بَلْ أَنتُم بِهَدِيَّتِكُمْ تَفْرَحُونَ {النمل/36} ارْجِعْ إِلَيْهِمْ فَلَنَأْتِيَنَّهُمْ بِجُنُودٍ لَّا قِبَلَ لَهُم بِهَا وَلَنُخْرِجَنَّهُم مِّنْهَا أَذِلَّةً وَهُمْ صَاغِرُونَ {النمل/37}

In the above case, there are two countries one may refer to with today's terminologies. They are the kingdom of Sulayman as and Balqis.

The approach of Sulayman as is to be deterrent but not really with the purpose of attack. If Sulayman as wanted, then he did not need to send a messenger to Balqis but rather could immediately attack their country. Yet, Sulayman as displays a very firm position of deterrence to cause them to reconsider their position.

On the other hand, the generals of Balqis, in today's terms, support Balqis in a case of physical attack by expressing قَالُوا نَحْنُ أُوْلُوا قُوَّةٍ وَأُولُوا بَأْسٍ شَدِيدٍ.

Yet, Balqis as an intelligent leader knows the consequences of a deterrent real power as she mentions[45] قَالَتْ إِنَّ الْمُلُوكَ إِذَا دَخَلُوا قَرْيَةً أَفْسَدُوهَا وَجَعَلُوا أَعِزَّةَ أَهْلِهَا أَذِلَّةً وَكَذَلِكَ يَفْعَلُونَ {النمل/34}. This knowledge of Balqis can be considered as ilmal yaqín.

---

44. 29. She said, "O eminent ones, indeed, to me has been delivered a noble letter. 30. Indeed, it is from Solomon, and indeed, it reads: 'In the name of Allah ﷻ, the Entirely Merciful, the Especially Merciful, 31. Be not haughty with me but come to me in submission [as Muslims].' "32. She said, "O eminent ones, advise me in my affair. I would not decide a matter until you witness [for] me."33. They said, "We are men of strength and of great military might, but the command is yours, so see what you will command."34. She said, "Indeed kings—when they enter a city, they ruin it and render the honored of its people humbled. And thus do they do. 35. But indeed, I will send to them a gift and see with what [reply] the messengers will return."36. So when they came to Solomon, he said, "Do you provide me with wealth? But what Allah ﷻ has given me is better than what He has given you. Rather, it is you who rejoice in your gift. 37. Return to them, for we will surely come to them with soldiers that they will be powerless to encounter, and we will surely expel them therefrom in humiliation, and they will be debased."

45. She said, "Indeed kings—when they enter a city, they ruin it and render the honored of its people humbled. And thus do they do.

Yet, she wants to investigate further this reality of firm deterrence of Sulayman as by sending him gifts as mentioned[46] وَإِنِّي مُرْسِلَةٌ إِلَيْهِم بِهَدِيَّةٍ فَنَاظِرَةٌ بِمَ يَرْجِعُ الْمُرْسَلُونَ {النمل/35}.

These messengers of Balqis face the reality of Sulayman as with firm deterrence as[47] فَلَمَّا جَاء سُلَيْمَانَ قَالَ أَتُمِدُّونَنِ بِمَالٍ فَمَا آتَانِيَ اللَّهُ خَيْرٌ مِّمَّا آتَاكُم بَلْ أَنتُم بِهَدِيَّتِكُمْ تَفْرَحُونَ {النمل/36} ارْجِعْ إِلَيْهِمْ فَلَنَأْتِيَنَّهُمْ بِجُنُودٍ لَّا قِبَلَ لَهُم بِهَا وَلَنُخْرِجَنَّهُم مِّنْهَا أَذِلَّةً وَهُمْ صَاغِرُونَ {النمل/37}. The knowledge of Balqis can be considered as 'aynal yaqín at this stage.

Finally, Balqis goes herself to face the reality of power of Sulayman as as mentioned[48]
فَلَمَّا جَاءتْ قِيلَ أَهَكَذَا عَرْشُكِ قَالَتْ كَأَنَّهُ هُوَ وَأُوتِينَا الْعِلْمَ مِن قَبْلِهَا وَكُنَّا مُسْلِمِينَ {النمل/42}.

In this case, one of the first displays of power of Sulayman as is the mention of[49] عَرْشُكِ which shows her intimate circle being known and monitored by Sulayman as. This shows the intelligence power of Sulayman as in that he can have access to the most inner circle of her kingdom. When Balqis sees this, she mentions her position of being a Muslim with ilmal yaqín as mentioned[50] وَأُوتِينَا الْعِلْمَ مِن قَبْلِهَا وَكُنَّا مُسْلِمِينَ.

When she experiences and tastes the reality of the power of Sulayman as with haqqal yaqín as mentioned[51] قِيلَ لَهَا ادْخُلِي الصَّرْحَ فَلَمَّا رَأَتْهُ حَسِبَتْهُ لُجَّةً وَكَشَفَتْ عَن سَاقَيْهَا قَالَ إِنَّهُ صَرْحٌ مُّمَرَّدٌ مِّن قَوَارِيرَ, then she embraces Islam fully as mentioned قَالَتْ رَبِّ إِنِّي ظَلَمْتُ نَفْسِي وَأَسْلَمْتُ مَعَ سُلَيْمَانَ لِلَّهِ رَبِّ الْعَالَمِينَ {النمل/44}.

Similarly, if a person knows the consequences of his or her choices in one's life in one's relationship with Allah ﷻ he or she may reconsider

---

46. But indeed, I will send to them a gift and see with what [reply] the messengers will return."
47. 36. So when they came to Solomon, he said, "Do you provide me with wealth? But what Allah has given me is better than what He has given you. Rather, it is you who rejoice in your gift. 37. Return to them, for we will surely come to them with soldiers that they will be powerless to encounter, and we will surely expel them therefrom in humiliation, and they will be debased."
48. So when she arrived, it was said [to her], "Is your throne like this?" She said, "[It is] as though it was it." [Solomon said], "And we were given knowledge before her, and we have been Muslims [in submission to Allah ﷻ].
49. your throne
50. "And we were given knowledge before her, and we have been Muslims [in submission to Allah ﷻ].
51. She was told, "Enter the palace." But when she saw it, she thought it was a body of water and uncovered her shins [to wade through]. He said, "Indeed, it is a palace [whose floor is] made smooth with glass." She said, "My Lord, indeed I have wronged myself, and I submit with Solomon to Allah ﷻ, Lord of the worlds."

one's disposition and stop one's abusive and oppressive relationship with one's own real self due to one's lack of recognition, purposefully acting blind, ungrateful, and unappreciative in one's relationship with Rabbul A'lamin.

In a similar sense, Allahu A'lam, it is possible that a kãfir or a person can experience three levels of punishment in one's life with ilmal yaqín, aynal yaqín and haqqal yaqín. These punishments can display in one's life through different trials, tests, difficulties, sicknesses, and fears.

This can be analyzed with the critical word لَنَبْلُوَنَّكُمْ mentioned in the Qurãn as:

وَلَنَبْلُوَنَّكُمْ بِشَيْءٍ مِّنَ الْخَوفْ وَالْجُوعِ وَنَقْصٍ مِّنَ الأَمَوَالِ وَالأنفُسِ وَالثَّمَرَاتِ وَبَشِّرِ الصَّابِرِينَ {البقرة/155}[52]

إِنَّا جَعَلْنَا مَا عَلَى الْأَرْضِ زِينَةً لَّهَا لِنَبْلُوَهُمْ أَيُّهُمْ أَحْسَنُ عَمَلًا {الكهف/7}[53]

كُلُّ نَفْسٍ ذَائِقَةُ الْمَوْتِ وَنَبْلُوكُم بِالشَّرِّ وَالْخَيْرِ فِتْنَةً وَإِلَيْنَا تُرْجَعُونَ {الأنبياء/35}[54]

وَلَنَبْلُوَنَّكُمْ حَتَّى نَعْلَمَ الْمُجَاهِدِينَ مِنكُمْ وَالصَّابِرِينَ وَنَبْلُوَ أَخْبَارَكُمْ {محمد/31}[55]

After all of the above knowledge of seeing and tasting different punishments in this life, if the kãfir still chooses the kufr, then his or her final and continuous abode can be punishment in the afterlife. May Allah ﷻ protect us.

On the other hand, the above different levels of difficulties can be the means to increase the level of a believer in his or her relationship with Allah ﷻ.

After all of the above knowledge of seeing and tasting, if the mu'min still chooses the sin, then his or her temporal abode can be punishment in the afterlife. May Allah ﷻ protect us.

If one thinks the opposite, such as the existence of Jahannam is to punish people, then Allah ﷻ does not really need any means or tools

---

52. And We will surely test you with something of fear and hunger and a loss of wealth and lives and fruits, but give good tidings to the patient,
53. Indeed, We have made that which is on the earth adornment for it that We may test them [as to] which of them is best in deed.
54. Every soul will taste death. And We test you with evil and with good as trial; and to Us you will be returned.
55. And We will surely test you until We make evident those who strive among you [for the cause of Allah ﷻ] and the patient, and We will test your affairs.

such as Jahannam to punish the creation that Allah ﷻ has created. If Allah ﷻ wanted, all of the creation can be terminated immediately as mentioned[56] وَنُفِخَ فِي الصُّورِ فَصَعِقَ مَن فِي السَّمَاوَاتِ وَمَن فِي الْأَرْضِ إِلَّا مَن شَاءَ اللَّهُ ثُمَّ نُفِخَ فِيهِ أُخْرَىٰ فَإِذَا هُم قِيَامٌ يَنظُرُونَ {الزمر/68}. Yet, the existence of Jahannam has a purpose and wisdom.

In that sense, the detailed description of Jahannam is explained in the Qurãn possibly, to deter and convince the person with their faculties of mind and emotions in order for them to really and carefully reconsider their choice and course of actions.

In a similar sense, the wisdom in the laws of Islãm of having an army in a country is to deter the people or groups from any type of aggressive and oppressive action towards them as mentioned[57] وَأَعِدُّوا لَهُم مَّا اسْتَطَعْتُم مِّن قُوَّةٍ وَمِن رِّبَاطِ الْخَيْلِ تُرْهِبُونَ بِهِ عَدُوَّ اللَّهِ وَعَدُوَّكُمْ وَآخَرِينَ مِن دُونِهِمْ لَا تَعْلَمُونَهُمُ اللَّهُ يَعْلَمُهُمْ وَمَا تُنفِقُوا مِن شَيْءٍ فِي سَبِيلِ اللَّهِ يُوَفَّ إِلَيْكُمْ وَأَنتُمْ لَا تُظْلَمُونَ {الأنفال/60}.

In this sense, the laws of Islam prohibit using the power merely to terminate, kill, and cause chaos on earth. The existence or display of power with preparation is to deter the evil-doers from their possible evil choices, Allahu A'lam.

It is critical to realize that these oppressive and aggressive engagements can come from unexpected directions or perspectives as mentioned[58] لَا تَعْلَمُونَهُمُ. Yet, as a way of following the means, the person follows the causality, means, and makes tawakkul to Allah ﷻ after making some preparations and leave the results to Allah ﷻ as mentioned[59] اللَّهُ يَعْلَمُهُمْ.

Manifestations of Wisdom & Power: This Life and Afterlife

When we consider the difficulties in the world, they may follow a cyclical process of ease and difficulty. In the akhirah, this ease cycle may not be necessarily be the case. May Allah ﷻ protect us, Amìn.

---

56. And the Horn will be blown, and whoever is in the heavens and whoever is on the earth will fall dead except whom Allah ﷻ wills. Then it will be blown again, and at once they will be standing, looking on.
57. And prepare against them whatever you are able of power and of steeds of war by which you may terrify the enemy of Allah ﷻ and your enemy and others besides them whom you do not know [but] whom Allah ﷻ knows. And whatever you spend in the cause of Allah ﷻ will be fully repaid to you, and you will not be wronged.
58. You do not know
59. [but] whom Allah ﷻ knows

In the akhirah, there is the manifestation of power, qudrah. The manifestation of hikmah can be secondary. The means or reasons covering the realities may not have substance in the akhirah as compared to the cases in this world. In the life of the world, the manifestation of hikmah, wisdom can be prominent. The means or reasons cover the realities.

In this sense, in the akhirah, both the punishments and the pleasures are personalized. In the world, they can be generalized due to the cover of reasons and means. The punishments or pleasures can have an overall effect and influence. This is mentioned in[60] وَاتَّقُوا فِتْنَةً لَّا تُصِيبَنَّ الَّذِينَ ظَلَمُوا مِنكُمْ خَاصَّةً وَاعْلَمُوا أَنَّ اللَّهَ شَدِيدُ الْعِقَابِ {الأنفال/25}.

Hasad: The Internal Enemy

When we analyze the ayah[61] وَإِن كُنتُمْ فِي رَيْبٍ مِّمَّا نَزَّلْنَا عَلَى عَبْدِنَا فَأْتُوا بِسُورَةٍ مِّن مِّثْلِهِ, the early society of Meccans seemed to make claims and argue about two objections. One was related with the Qurãn. In this case of objection, we discussed how the Qurãn has made an open challenge and their arguments have all been abolished and disabled. There has not really been a case about the survival of this objection. This objection has faded very quickly.

The other was by bringing arguments criticizing, astagfirullah, why Rasulullah ﷺ was chosen as a prophet but not others.

In this latter case, the problem was related with hasad, envy. Envy is a feeling of discontented or resentful longing aroused by someone else's given or earned possession and qualities [2].

This feeling of hasad can consume the person as mentioned [6] by Rasulullah ﷺ. This consuming feeling can cause the person to have constant bad feelings about and be envious of others. The envious, consumed person can then transform his or her feelings into harming others by looks, words, and actions. Allah SWT mentions this in the Quran with its protection dua as[62] وَمِن شَرِّ حَاسِدٍ إِذَا حَسَدَ {الفلق/5}.

When the damage due to envy is done through eyes, then it is called nazar or the evil eye. This can really damage the targeted person of the

60. And fear a trial which will not strike those who have wronged among you exclusively, and know that Allah ﷻ is severe in penalty.
61. And if you are in doubt about what We have sent down upon Our Servant [Muhammad ﷺ], then produce a surah the like thereof
62. And from the evil of an envier when he envies."

envious person. One can imagine in that sense an envious person is boiling poisonous full of emotions in oneself. Then, its release can come through the eyes.

The second form of display of hasad or envy is through words. In this case, slandering and backbiting can be considered as some of the branching displays of hasad in different forms. Generally, the person slanders and backbites the person whom they envy or feel hasad.

The third form of display of hasad or envy can be through actions. In this case, greed and covetousness can be some of the branching displays of hasad in actions in different forms. The envious person wants to hold on to everything, be stingy, and not share in order to deprive others of the same bounty given by Allah SWT.

How to Cope with Hasad

Hasad generally presents with the people who understand the value of something that another person has. They get angry about it because they don't have it but another person or people do have it.

Yet, there are a lot of things in life that can explicitly show that they are given by Allah ﷻ to the person with a Fadl and Rahmah from Allah ﷻ. In this sense, hasad also shows a sense of displeasure with the choice of Allah ﷻ. May Allah ﷻ protect us, Amìn.

An intelligent and wise person recognizes this God-given ability and choice to another person. Then, after acknowledging it, he or she still maintains the position of gratitude and appreciation in their own positions with Allah ﷻ. At the same time, he or she respects the choice of Allah ﷻ . Then, at the highest level, she or he may try to learn and benefit from this person who has this privilege given by Allah ﷻ.

If we analyze the ayahs of the Qurãn, one can find different forms of this disposition. For example,[63] وَدَّ كَثِيرٌ مِّنْ أَهْلِ الْكِتَابِ لَوْ يَرُدُّونَكُم مِّن بَعْدِ إِيمَانِكُمْ كُفَّاراً حَسَدًا مِّنْ عِندِ أَنفُسِهِم مِّن بَعْدِ مَا تَبَيَّنَ لَهُمُ الْحَقُّ فَاعْفُواْ وَاصْفَحُواْ حَتَّى يَأْتِيَ اللّهُ بِأَمْرِهِ إِنَّ اللّهَ عَلَى كُلِّ شَيْءٍ قَدِيرٌ. {البقرة/109}

Ahlu Kitãb is familiar with the scriptures from Allah ﷻ. They can have a very good understanding about the value of the Qurãn

63. Many of the People of the Scripture wish they could turn you back to disbelief after you have believed, out of envy from themselves [even] after the truth has become clear to them. So pardon and overlook until Allah ﷻ delivers His command. Indeed, Allah ﷻ is over all things competent.

and Rasulullah ﷺ compared to the people who may not have much understanding about the scriptures.

In this regard, a person who knows about the value of the Qurãn and Rasulullah ﷺ has the potential to make hasad as mentioned وَدَّ كَثِيرٌ مِّنْ أَهْلِ الْكِتَابِ لَوْ يَرُدُّونَكُم مِّن بَعْدِ إِيمَانِكُمْ كُفَّاراً حَسَدًا مِّنْ عِندِ أَنفُسِهِم مِّن بَعْدِ مَا تَبَيَّنَ لَهُمُ الْحَقُّ.

Yet, instead of benefitting and learning from the full, all-inclusive, and authentic scripture- the Qurãn- they spiritually kill and consume themselves in identity dynamics resulting from hasad. They know the Qurãn and Rasulullah ﷺ so well as mentioned[64] بَعْدِ مَا تَبَيَّنَ لَهُمُ الْحَقُّ and[65] لَّذِينَ آتَيْنَاهُمُ الْكِتَابَ يَعْرِفُونَهُ كَمَا يَعْرِفُونَ أَبْنَاءهُمُ الَّذِينَ خَسِرُواْ أَنفُسَهُمْ فَهُمْ لاَ يُؤْمِنُونَ {الأنعام/20}.

Yet, they don't benefit and learn from this fresh, complete, and authentic source—the Qurãn and Rasulullah ﷺ—due to their hasad as mentioned حَسَدًا مِّنْ عِندِ أَنفُسِهِم.

Their hasad forces them to desire this bounty of Allah ﷻ given to Muslims to be lost, to vanish, and to become disoriented as mentioned[66] وَدَّ كَثِيرٌ مِّنْ أَهْلِ الْكِتَابِ لَوْ يَرُدُّونَكُم مِّن بَعْدِ إِيمَانِكُمْ كُفَّاراً

Therefore, one can understand when a person who is a so-called Muslim becomes a lunatic about his or her religion or when he or she claims to have left Islam, one can immediately witness these cases in public receiving great focus from media attention. These efforts can be due to the display of the inner burning lust of departure of Muslims from the Qurãn and sunnah as mentioned يَرُدُّونَكُم stemming from consuming hasad.

Another example is[67] أَلَمْ تَرَ إِلَى الَّذِينَ أُوتُواْ نَصِيبًا مِّنَ الْكِتَابِ يُؤْمِنُونَ بِالْجِبْتِ وَالطَّاغُوتِ وَيَقُولُونَ لِلَّذِينَ كَفَرُواْ هَؤُلاء أَهْدَى مِنَ الَّذِينَ آمَنُواْ سَبِيلاً {النساء/51}.

---

64. After you have believed
65. Those to whom We have given the Scripture recognize it as they recognize their [own] sons. Those who will lose themselves [in the Hereafter] do not believe.
66. Many of the People of the Scripture wish they could turn you back to disbelief after you have believed
67. 51. Have you not seen those who were given a portion of the Scripture, who believe in superstition and false objects of worship and say about the disbelievers, "These are better guided than the believers as to the way"? 52. Those are the ones whom Allah ﷻ has cursed; and he whom Allah ﷻ curses—never will you find for him a helper. 53. Or have they a share of dominion? Then [if that were so], they would not give the people [even as much as] the speck on a date seed. 54. Or do they envy people for what Allah ﷻ has given them of His bounty? But we had already given the family of Abraham the Scripture and wisdom and conferred upon them a great kingdom. 55. And some among them believed in it, and some among them were averse to it. And sufficient is Hell as a blaze.

أُولَئِكَ الَّذِينَ لَعَنَهُمُ اللهُ وَمَن يَلْعَنِ اللهُ فَلَن تَجِدَ لَهُ نَصِيرًا {النساء/52} أَمْ لَهُمْ نَصِيبٌ مِّنَ الْمُلْكِ فَإِذًا لاَّ يُؤْتُونَ النَّاسَ نَقِيرًا {النساء/53} أَمْ يَحْسُدُونَ النَّاسَ عَلَى مَا آتَاهُمُ اللهُ مِن فَضْلِهِ فَقَدْ آتَيْنَا آلَ إِبْرَاهِيمَ الْكِتَابَ وَالْحِكْمَةَ وَآتَيْنَاهُم مُّلْكًا عَظِيمًا {النساء/54} فَمِنْهُم مَّنْ آمَنَ بِهِ وَمِنْهُم مَّن صَدَّ عَنْهُ وَكَفَى بِجَهَنَّمَ سَعِيرًا {النساء/55}

According to tafsirul wahidi (rh) [7], مِنْهُم in the ayah فَمِنْهُم مَّنْ آمَنَ بِهِ وَمِنْهُم مَّن صَدَّ عَنْهُ وَكَفَى بِجَهَنَّمَ سَعِيرًا {النساء/55} refers to Ahlu-Kitāb. In this regard, the expression أَلَمْ تَرَ إِلَى الَّذِينَ أُوتُواْ نَصِيبًا مِّنَ الْكِتَابِ can also indicate Ahlu-Kitāb. Referring to our original discussion, when a person or group knows the value of anything, they have the potential of making hasad as mentioned أَمْ يَحْسُدُونَ النَّاسَ عَلَى مَا آتَاهُمُ اللهُ مِن فَضْلِهِ.

Here, the word النَّاسَ can also indicate any person who has the potential of making hasad.

In this regard, one of the clear and explicit choices of Allah ﷻ is the family of Ibrahim as فَقَدْ آتَيْنَا آلَ إِبْرَاهِيمَ الْكِتَابَ وَالْحِكْمَةَ وَآتَيْنَاهُم مُّلْكًا عَظِيمًا {النساء/54}.

Yet, no one has the right to make hasad about this choosiness by Allah ﷻas mentioned in[68] {الدخان/32} وَلَقَدِ اخْتَرْنَاهُمْ عَلَى عِلْمٍ عَلَى الْعَالَمِينَ.

In all of the choices of Allah ,ﷻ there is a hikmah, knowledge, and reason as mentioned عَلَى عِلْمٍ in the ayah.

These reasons and this wisdom can be known by the people of Allah ﷻ. The ones who don't understand should humbly and respectfully submit themselves to the choices of Allah ﷻ.

If the person or group does not understand the value of something, then there may not really be hasad. The ayah[69] سَيَقُولُ الْمُخَلَّفُونَ إِذَا انطَلَقْتُمْ إِلَى مَغَانِمَ لِتَأْخُذُوهَا ذَرُونَا نَتَّبِعْكُمْ يُرِيدُونَ أَن يُبَدِّلُوا كَلَامَ اللهِ قُل لَّن تَتَّبِعُونَا كَذَلِكُمْ قَالَ اللهُ مِن قَبْلُ فَسَيَقُولُونَ بَلْ تَحْسُدُونَنَا بَلْ كَانُوا لَا يَفْقَهُونَ إِلَّا قَلِيلًا {الفتح/15} can show this perspective.

The hypocrites blame the believers claiming that Muslims are doing hasad of them as mentioned .بَلْ تَحْسُدُونَنَا Yet, real believers truly understand the real value of everything. They don't make hasad of the hypocrites. The level of hypocrites is so low. Hasad requires knowing the real value of everything as mentioned[70] {الفتح/15} بَلْ كَانُوا لَا يَفْقَهُونَ إِلَّا قَلِيلًا.

---

68. And We certainly chose them by knowledge over [all] the worlds.

69. Those who remained behind will say when you set out toward the war booty to take it, "Let us follow you." They wish to change the words of Allah ﷻ. Say, "Never will you follow us. Thus did Allah say before." So they will say, "Rather, you envy us." But [in fact] they were not understanding except a little.

70. But [in fact] they were not understanding except a little.

Realistic & Powerful Teachings of the Qurãn

When we analyze the Qurãn, there are a lot of styles and perspectives moving the emotions of the readers. Yet, when a message or teaching arrives to teach and convince people, humans tend to use their faculties of mind, intellect, and reason to make a substantial and permanent choice. In other words, one can say that life-changing decisions and choices cannot be made purely with emotions.

In this regard, one can truly realize the constant, emerging engagement of the Qurãn with the reader through the faculties of mind, reason, and realities. In other words, one can consider emotions to be transient or temporary. Therefore, the Qurãn engages the person by using one's logical faculties to make a proper and determined choice.

Yet, when the message is so convincing and logical, then the style of delivery of these precise, coherent, and realistic teachings can stimulate both the reader's mind and heart.

If there is a piece of text in philosophy, it may stimulate only one's intellect and mind.

If there is a piece of text in literature, it may stimulate only and mostly one's emotions and heart.

Yet, the Qurãn very realistically and objectively addresses both the mind and the heart of the person with precision and coherence, SubhanAllah.

In this sense, the experts of logic—such as scholars of kalam—can be overwhelmed with the precision and coherence of the Qurãn engaging fully with the mind, reason, and intellect. On the other hand, the experts of experiential knowledge- such as the scholars of tasawwuf- can be overwhelmed with the convoluted openings of the Qurãn engaging fully with the emotions and experiences. Yet, balance comes when one approaches the Qurãn with both perspectives.

At the same time, the Qurãn directly addresses all of the faculties of the heart and spirituality generating different emotions. In this sense, emotions are peaked with reality but not exaggerated as in the cases of poets as mentioned[71]

71. 224. And the poets—[only] the deviators follow them; 225. Do you not see that in every valley they roam 226. And that they say what they do not do? -

وَالشُّعَرَاء يَتَّبِعُهُمُ الْغَاوُونَ {الشعراء/224} أَلَمْ تَرَ أَنَّهُمْ فِي كُلِّ وَادٍ يَهِيمُونَ {الشعراء/225} وَأَنَّهُمْ يَقُولُونَ مَا لَا يَفْعَلُونَ {الشعراء/226}.

The miracle of the Qurãn moves all of the faculties of heart and mind with emotions, logic, and reason of reality and objectivity.

Different Style of the Qurãn according to the Topic

The Qurãn uses different styles according to the topic. For example, one can view the descriptions of the Qurãn regarding the yawmul qiyamah, apocalypse. The reality of yawmal qiyamah is beyond full human understanding. The style used in the Qurãn depicts this reality so powerfully that the emotions, mind, and heart all move with the strong and beautiful motifs of the descriptions. The descriptions use human words in the macro and micro cosmos in a series of events beyond the usual human usage of language. For example, one can analyze the ayahs such as[72] إِذَا الشَّمْسُ كُوِّرَتْ {التكوير/1} وَإِذَا النُّجُومُ انكَدَرَتْ {التكوير/2} وَإِذَا الْجِبَالُ سُيِّرَتْ {التكوير/3} وَإِذَا الْعِشَارُ عُطِّلَتْ {التكوير/4} وَإِذَا الْوُحُوشُ حُشِرَتْ {التكوير/5} وَإِذَا الْبِحَارُ سُجِّرَتْ {التكوير/6} وَإِذَا النُّفُوسُ زُوِّجَتْ {التكوير/7} وَإِذَا الْمَوْؤُودَةُ سُئِلَتْ {التكوير/8} بِأَيِّ ذَنبٍ قُتِلَتْ {التكوير/9} وَإِذَا الصُّحُفُ نُشِرَتْ {التكوير/10} وَإِذَا السَّمَاء كُشِطَتْ {التكوير/11} وَإِذَا الْجَحِيمُ سُعِّرَتْ {التكوير/12} وَإِذَا الْجَنَّةُ أُزْلِفَتْ {التكوير/13} عَلِمَتْ نَفْسٌ مَّا أَحْضَرَتْ {التكوير/14}

Another example is[73] إِذَا السَّمَاء انفَطَرَتْ {الإنفطار/1} وَإِذَا الْكَوَاكِبُ انتَثَرَتْ {الإنفطار/2} وَإِذَا الْبِحَارُ فُجِّرَتْ {الإنفطار/3} وَإِذَا الْقُبُورُ بُعْثِرَتْ {الإنفطار/4} عَلِمَتْ نَفْسٌ مَّا قَدَّمَتْ وَأَخَّرَتْ {الإنفطار/5}.

On the other hand, if one reviews the language of the Qurãn regarding inheritance, there is a need for plain and explicit language without much implicit implementations for other interpretations. This style, in this sense, blocks misuse and abuse of the teachings especially in the cases of social and personal rights. One can analyze the ayahs

72. 1. When the sun is wrapped up [in darkness] 2. And when the stars fall, dispersing, 3. And when the mountains are removed 4. And when full-term she-camels are neglected 5 And when the wild beasts are gathered.6. And when the seas are filled with flame 7. And when the souls are paired 8. And when the girl [who was] buried alive is asked 9. For what sin she was killed 10. And when the pages are made public 11. And when the sky is stripped away 12. And when Hellfire is set ablaze 13. And when Paradise is brought near, 14. A soul will [then] know what it has brought [with it].

73. 1. When the sky breaks apart 2. And when the stars fall, scattering, 3. And when the seas are erupted 4. And when the [contents of] graves are scattered, 5. A soul will [then] know what it has put forth and kept back.

such as[74] يُوصِيكُمُ اللهُ فِي أَوْلَادِكُمْ لِلذَّكَرِ مِثْلُ حَظِّ الأُنثَيَيْنِ فَإِن كُنَّ نِسَاء فَوْقَ اثْنَتَيْنِ فَلَهُنَّ ثُلُثَا مَا تَرَكَ وَإِن كَانَتْ وَاحِدَةً فَلَهَا النِّصْفُ وَلأَبَوَيْهِ لِكُلِّ وَاحِدٍ مِّنْهُمَا السُّدُسُ مِمَّا تَرَكَ إِن كَانَ لَهُ وَلَدٌ فَإِن لَّمْ يَكُن لَّهُ وَلَدٌ وَوَرِثَهُ أَبَوَاهُ فَلأُمِّهِ الثُّلُثُ فَإِن كَانَ لَهُ إِخْوَةٌ فَلأُمِّهِ السُّدُسُ مِن بَعْدِ وَصِيَّةٍ يُوصِي بِهَا أَوْ دَيْنٍ آبَاؤُكُمْ وَأَبناؤُكُمْ لاَ تَدْرُونَ أَيُّهُمْ أَقْرَبُ لَكُمْ نَفْعاً فَرِيضَةً مِّنَ اللهِ إِنَّ اللهَ كَانَ عَلِيما حَكِيمًا {النساء/11}.

One of the distinct features of the Qurãn is its unchanging perfection and completeness.

When a person reviews any book written in any field, the author or a group of experts needs to revise it constantly and produce different editions. One can even find this approach in literature. Some of the connoisseurs and expert poets revise their own works in poetry after many years. As they look at their work later, they may find it to be dull and inefficient at conveying the message that they want to deliver.

Yet, the Qurãn is perfect and complete as the Qurãn is from Allah ﷻ.

One of the unique features of the Qurãn is that the Qurãn displays perfection and completeness in all the fields and not just in one part. When one reviews the poets at the time of Jahiliyyah, before Islam, one can find a lot of expert poets on different topics. Perhaps a poet can write expertly on one topic, such as love. Yet, when he or she writes on courage, his or her poems can seem to lose value. Yet, the Qurãn shows completeness and perfection in all fields on all different topics.

When one reviews the style of the Qurãn, one can truly realize this distinction in every surãh, in every ayah, and in the usage of each and every word. For example, when one goes back to the beginning of this sûrah as[75] الم {البقرة/1} ذَلِكَ الْكِتَابُ لاَ رَيْبَ فِيهِ هُدًى لِّلْمُتَّقِينَ {البقرة/2}, one can realize that this is a very distinct style. Then, the beginning of the sûrah indicate this distinction, uniqueness, and challenging style with ذَلِكَ الْكِتَابُ

74. Allah ﷻ instructs you concerning your children: for the male, what is equal to the share of two females. But if there are [only] daughters, two or more, for them is two thirds of one's estate. And if there is only one, for her is half. And for one's parents, to each one of them is a sixth of his estate if he left children. But if he had no children and the parents [alone] inherit from him, then for his mother is one third. And if he had brothers [or sisters], for his mother is a sixth, after any bequest he [may have] made or debt. Your parents or your children—you know not which of them are nearest to you in benefit. [These shares are] an obligation [imposed] by Allah ﷻ. Indeed, Allah ﷻ is ever Knowing and Wise.

75. 1. Alif, Lam, Meem. 2. This is the Book about which there is no doubt, a guidance for those conscious of Allah ﷻ -

{البقرة/2} لاَ رَيْبَ فِيهِ هُدًى لِّلْمُتَّقِينَ. Yet, at the same time the current ayah as[76] وَإِن كُنتُمْ فِي رَيْبٍ مِّمَّا نَزَّلْنَا عَلَى عَبْدِنَا فَأْتُواْ بِسُورَةٍ مِّن مِّثْلِهِ وَادْعُواْ شُهَدَاءكُم مِّن دُونِ اللّهِ إِنْ كُنْتُمْ صَادِقِينَ {البقرة/23} فَإِن لَّمْ تَفْعَلُواْ وَلَن تَفْعَلُواْ فَاتَّقُواْ النَّارَ الَّتِي وَقُودُهَا النَّاسُ وَالْحِجَارَةُ أُعِدَّتْ لِلْكَافِرِينَ {البقرة/24} also represents this distinction, uniqueness, and challenging style. One can realize that each ayah of the Qurãn as well as the ayahs within a sûrah and the words used in different combinations have relationships.

On the other hand, if a person does not really analyze and approach the Qurãn with this critical and wholistic approach, he or she may not benefit as much.

It is interesting to realize that after the teachings of imãn and 'ibadah, Allah ﷻ mentions the department of prophethood and messengership in the institution of religion. In other words, one cannot truly imagine, understand, and be in the institution of a religion without a teacher referred to as prophet.

As humans, we need practical examples of how to apply the teachings of religion in our everyday life. All prophets and Rasulullah ﷺ model this implementation for us as examples. The claims of the people not valuing the teachings of Rasulullah ﷺ are all temporary lived attempts that don't have sustainability. They emerge sometimes and then fade away. They emerge other times and again fade away.

Causality & Mercy of Allah ﷻ

When we analyze the expression[77], {البقرة/24} أُعِدَّتْ لِلْكَافِرِينَ one can realize an important style of the Qurãn. The Qurãn presents especially that the result of an incident or a person's retribution or reward is related to a cause. It is not a haphazard or random result, but there is a cause for this ending.

In this case, the reason for punishment as mentioned[78] فَاتَّقُواْ النَّارَ الَّتِي وَقُودُهَا النَّاسُ وَالْحِجَارَةُ is due to the kufr as mentioned[79] .أُعِدَّتْ لِلْكَافِرِينَ Kufr is the cause of punishment.

76. 23. And if you are in doubt about what We have sent down upon Our Servant [Muhammad ﷺ], then produce a surah the like thereof and call upon your witnesses other than Allah ﷻ, if you should be truthful. 24. But if you do not—and you will never be able to—then fear the Fire, whose fuel is men and stones, prepared for the disbelievers.
77. prepared for the disbelievers.
78. then fear the Fire, whose fuel is men and stones
79. prepared for the disbelievers.

In many places in the Qurãn and Hadith, Allah ﷻ mentions the Rahmah of Allah ﷻ in the cases of deserved punishment of a person due to a cause. In other words, the punishment is there due to the cause of the person's choice. The reason for punishment is not really to make the person suffer, have pain, and be in agony. The mentioning of the Names of Allah ﷻ as al-Gafûr and ar-Rahìm after the mentioning of the punishment can very obviously allude to this reality in many places in the Qurãn and in the sunnah of Rasulullah ﷺ.

For example,[80] وَمَن لَّمْ يُؤْمِن بِاللَّهِ وَرَسُولِهِ فَإِنَّا أَعْتَدْنَا لِلْكَافِرِينَ سَعِيرًا {الفتح/13} وَلِلَّهِ مُلْكُ السَّمَاوَاتِ وَالْأَرْضِ يَغْفِرُ لِمَن يَشَاءُ وَيُعَذِّبُ مَن يَشَاءُ وَكَانَ اللَّهُ غَفُورًا رَّحِيمًا {الفتح/14}

The position of the kufr is mentioned with وَمَن لَّمْ يُؤْمِن بِاللَّهِ وَرَسُولِهِ. The cause of kufr is connected to the choice of a person and has a result and punishment as mentioned فَإِنَّا أَعْتَدْنَا لِلْكَافِرِينَ سَعِيرًا {الفتح/13}. Yet, the reality of this punishment is mentioned in the following ayah. This reality is not to put the person into pain and suffering. If Allah ﷻ orders, everything is under Allah ﷻ's Authority as mentioned وَلِلَّهِ مُلْكُ السَّمَاوَاتِ وَالْأَرْضِ.

The reality of this punishment is to make the person reconsider his or her position of false and wrong free will engagement and free choice. Then, the person is expected to ask forgiveness from Allah ﷻ as mentioned يَغْفِرُ لِمَن يَشَاءُ وَيُعَذِّبُ مَن يَشَاءُ وَكَانَ اللَّهُ غَفُورًا رَّحِيمًا {الفتح/14}.

In all approaches of the religion, Islãm, the Qurãn, and the teachings of Rasulullah ﷺ, one should really consider the maqãsid, the real purpose and goal.

Here the maqãsid is not to punish. Allah ﷻ owns everything as mentioned وَلِلَّهِ مُلْكُ السَّمَاوَاتِ وَالْأَرْضِ. Ownership does not require any type of logic and rationality in the discretion of how one should execute a decision about the owned item. This is mentioned as يَغْفِرُ لِمَن يَشَاءُ وَيُعَذِّبُ مَن يَشَاءُ.

Yet, in the Dominion of Allah ﷻ, Allah ﷻ gives us a share. From this Dominion of Allah ﷻ, Allah ﷻ addresses us as if we do not have any ownership. Allah ﷻ explains to us the causality, the reasons, and the results. Allah ﷻ reminds us of the dominant Attribute of Allah ﷻ as the Very and Most Merciful with وَكَانَ اللَّهُ غَفُورًا رَّحِيمًا although we deserve to be punished due to our own wrong choices.

May Allah ﷻ forgive us for our unappreciative behaviors, Amìn!

---

80. 13. And whoever has not believed in Allah ﷻ and His Messenger ﷺ—then indeed, We have prepared for the disbelievers a Blaze. 14. And to Allah ﷻ belongs the dominion of the heavens and the earth. He forgives whom He wills and punishes whom He wills. And ever is Allah ﷻ Forgiving and Merciful.

[25][81]

وَبَشِّرِ الَّذِين آمَنُواْ وَعَمِلُواْ الصَّالِحَاتِ أَنَّ لَهُمْ جَنَّاتٍ تَجْرِي مِن تَحْتِهَا الأَنْهَارُ كُلَّمَا رُزِقُواْ مِنْهَا مِن ثَمَرَةٍ رِّزْقاً قَالُواْ هَذَا الَّذِي رُزِقْنَا مِن قَبْلُ وَأُتُواْ بِهِ مُتَشَابِهاً وَلَهُمْ فِيهَا أَزْوَاجٌ مُّطَهَّرَةٌ وَهُمْ فِيهَا خَالِدُونَ {البقرة/25}

The earlier ayah sounds the call for everyone as[82] يَا أَيُّهَا النَّاسُ اعْبُدُواْ رَبَّكُمُ. The prior ayahs explain the possible choices of kuffār and munafiqs with[83] وَإِن كُنتُمْ فِي رَيْبٍ مِّمَّا نَزَّلْنَا عَلَى عَبْدِنَا. Then, the possible ending due to their wrong choice is warned and reminded to them with[84] فَاتَّقُواْ النَّارَ الَّتِي وَقُودُهَا النَّاسُ وَالْحِجَارَةُ أُعِدَّتْ لِلْكَافِرِينَ {البقرة/24}. Subsequently, this ayah emphasizes the position of the ones with the correct choices, purpose, and meaning in life as[85] وَبَشِّرِ الَّذِين آمَنُواْ وَعَمِلُواْ الصَّالِحَاتِ. Allahumma J'alna Minhum.

One of the interesting points of emphasis in this ayah is with the word مُتَشَابِهاً. As we live in an increasingly materialistic society, there are a lot of people who don't want to imagine further than they can experience with their 5 senses, and want to approach everything with the positivist worldview. In other words, a person may not make a choice and follow something if they cannot grasp it with his or her worldly materialistic means of the five senses. In this sense, a person who has this materialistic understanding can submit and make a choice if he or she knows what will be rewarded at the end of the deal. Therefore, the word مُتَشَابِهاً can give this materialistic conviction of the five senses although there is much more to be experienced than the senses of this world.

The expression[86] وَأُتُواْ بِهِ مُتَشَابِهاً can indicate another pleasure when the food is being served to the person. In other words, the majhul (passive) form of وَأُتُواْ with a practice of a food or drink served to the

81. And give good tidings to those who believe and do righteous deeds that they will have gardens [in Paradise] beneath which rivers flow. Whenever they are provided with a provision of fruit therefrom, they will say, "This is what we were provided with before." And it is given to them in likeness. And they will have therein purified spouses, and they will abide therein eternally.
82. O mankind, worship your Lord ﷻ
83. And if you are in doubt about what We have sent down upon Our Servant [Muhammad ﷺ]
84. then fear the Fire, whose fuel is men and stones, prepared for the disbelievers.
85. And give good tidings to those who believe and do righteous deeds
86. And it is given to them in likeness.

person can indicate another pleasure for the person besides the taste of the food itself.

Hope & Fear: Jannah & Jahannam

The symmetrical opposite of the ayah[87]

is فَاتَّقُواْ النَّارَ الَّتِي وَقُودُهَا النَّاسُ وَالْحِجَارَةُ أُعِدَّتْ لِلْكَافِرِينَ {البقرة/24}

وَبَشِّرِ الَّذِين آمَنُواْ وَعَمِلُواْ الصَّالِحَاتِ أَنَّ لَهُمْ جَنَّاتٍ{البقرة/25}

The existence of both Jannah and Jahannam has a purpose and wisdom. As humans, we have faculties of mind, intellect, and emotions that need to be fed with hope and optimism. At the same time, we have urges and potentials that need to be maintained and regulated with fear of real and full accountability.

Hope keeps the person constantly moving forward toward a goal with meaning and purpose.

Fear of accountability keeps the person away from abuse and oppression.

In this regard, if hope maintains the quantity, then fear maintains the quality.

Hope causes the person to engage in many good deeds as mentioned وَبَشِّرِ الَّذِين آمَنُواْ وَعَمِلُواْ الصَّالِحَاتِ أَنَّ لَهُمْ جَنَّاتٍ.

Fear causes the person reach for ikhlas and taqwa with intention as mentioned فَاتَّقُواْ النَّارَ الَّتِي وَقُودُهَا النَّاسُ وَالْحِجَارَةُ أُعِدَّتْ لِلْكَافِرِينَ.

Hope generates continuous action. Taqwa maintains ikhlas in intention.

Hope fuels entrepreneurship. Fear motivates sustainability and continuity.

Hope fuels the chivalry, futuwwah. Fear maintains the wisdom, hikmah.

87. 24. But if you do not—and you will never be able to—then fear the Fire, whose fuel is men and stones, prepared for the disbelievers. 25. And give good tidings to those who believe and do righteous deeds that they will have gardens [in Paradise]

Realities of Fear, Death, and Hope

When we look at both the philosophical and religious discourses of life and being, there is an anonymous agreement that everything that has a life has a beginning and an end, except Allah ﷻ. Therefore, Allah ﷻ is not similar to the creation as mentioned[88]

كُلُّ مَنْ عَلَيْهَا فَانٍ {الرحمن/26} وَيَبْقَى وَجْهُ رَبِّكَ ذُو الْجَلَالِ وَالْإِكْرَامِ {الرحمن/27}

Yet, as the name al-insãn can indicate, the humans are heedless and forgetful of this reality of death.

Forgetting death causes the person to increase their attachment to the temporal life with endless expectations.

Therefore, one of the true tests of imãn for a person is if they really want to meet with Allah ﷻ with death as mentioned[89]

قُلْ يَا أَيُّهَا الَّذِينَ هَادُوا إِن زَعَمْتُمْ أَنَّكُمْ أَوْلِيَاءُ لِلَّهِ مِن دُونِ النَّاسِ فَتَمَنَّوُا الْمَوْتَ إِن كُنتُمْ صَادِقِينَ {الجمعة/6}

If not, there is the high possibility of attachment to this life in a person even though the person seem to be very pious and religious.

If a person has the desire to die, this may be for different reasons.

One reason can be his or her suffering in this world and expecting a better life after death.

Another reason can be one's extreme desire to meet with Allah ﷻ.

Another reason can be to leave a good reputation behind among the living with one's death.

In all cases, a Muslim is prohibited to end his or her own life or the lives of others. Death comes with Divine Destiny, qadar or ajal.

Yet, above all, the possibilities of death can exist at the intentional or expectational levels.

The highest of these intentions is to keep and maintain the desire to meet with Allah ﷻ.

Sometimes, life becomes so burdensome with trials and tests that the person may not want to live anymore. This is also mentioned by

88. 26. And there will remain the Face of your Lord, Owner of Majesty and Honor. 27. And there will remain the Face of your Lord, Owner of Majesty and Honor.
89. Say, "O you who are Jews, if you claim that you are allies of Allah ﷻ, excluding the [other] people, then wish for death, if you should be truthful."

Rasulullah ﷺ- that people who are alive at the End of Times may envy the people in the grave because they are dead, thinking that they are fortunate. This is because of the amount of hardship at the End of Times.

Yet, with all evil-seeming incidents and the ugly-looking face of death, a person of Allah ﷻ referred to as awliyaullah, a person of بِسْمِ اللّٰهِ, and a person of imãn knows that death and evil-seeming incidents are only the means allowed, permitted, and created by Allah ﷻ.

In this sense, they don't get disturbed by current events or waylaid by any incident that instills fear, pessimism, and distraction from achieving their goal as existent beings.

On one side, they try to constantly increase their amazement of imãn and ma'rifatullah with yaqìn through both of the books of Allah ﷻ—the Qurãn and the universe. The universe is another book of Allah ﷻ to be read, analyzed, and explored with science through the lenses of imãn.

All of these explorations are performed through the guidance of al-hãdi, al-habìb, Rasulullah ﷺ.

On the other side, the people of imãn constantly give hope and breezes of imãn to everyone around them suffering from the choking depression of spiritual chaos and darkness, kufr especially during the times of fear and uncertainty.

Together they break through these dark layers of pessimism with hope and trust in Allah ﷻ by fully following the sunnah of Rasulullah ﷺ, al-mahdi.

Kufr and Imãn

A person of imãn has a different perspective on life than the person of kufr. The person of imãn can be in the same place, conditions, and time as the person of kufr. Yet, one can be in torture and the other can be in pleasure.

The person of iman can get the true meaning of everything by correctly relating everything to Allah ﷻ. The person of imãn knows that everything has a purpose, meaning, and is the servant of Allah ﷻ. Everything is a'bdullah. The person of iman lives a life of Jannah with dhikrullah, constantly remembering Allah ﷻ, the All-Powerful, the All in Control, the All Merciful and the All Caring.

On the other hand, the person of kufr sees everything as chaos, randomness, and purposeless. In this randomness, he or she gets scared by all the different possibilities of evil outcomes. He or she cracks his or her back under the burden of waswasa, and fear. Thinking of these possibilities and running to seek solutions to everything from everyone increases the fear in this person. The person of kufr lives a life of Jahannam in this world with all of those wrong assumptions.

A person of sound mind can ask, "Which path is preferred?" Anyone who has even a taste of sound mind would accept that imãn is not optional but required both for this world and the afterlife.

Iman leads to planning and preparation. Kufr involves no planning or preparation. A person of imãn makes preparation with 'ibadah. A person of kufr does not value 'ibadah and views it as unnecessary and a waste of time.

Meaning, Purpose, and 'Ibadah

Sometimes, we become confused by the means on the way toward the goal and purpose. When a person is traveling and trying to reach a destination, there can be good and bad scenes on the road. Yet, the purpose of the trip is to reach the destination without stopping and wasting time.

Similarly, different means such as work, family, and other engagements can cause the person to lose the purpose. A person very worried about his or her financial well-being or other worries can cause that person to lose the main purpose and meaning in life.

Rasulullah ﷺ teaches us to make the dua of اَللهُمَّ إنِّي أسْألُكَ الْعَفْوَ والْعَافِيَةَ فِيْ الدُّنْيَا وَالآخِرَةِ

"Allahumma inni asaluka afwa wal afiyah", [6].

Well-being is important. Yet, one should desire to have well-being in order to serve one's purpose and goal in life.

The purpose or goal is to make 'ibadah to Allah ﷻ. 'Ibadah is the expression of loving Allah ﷻ as the way the Prophet ﷺ practiced. Following Rasulullah ﷺ in all forms of 'ibadah and in all forms of life is the expression of love for Allah ﷻ and Rasulullah ﷺ.

Patience (Sabr) and Reliance (Tawakkul)

One of the hikmahs of 'ibadah is to teach us patience, sabr. When we say to each other to 'be patient', this trait is not something learned but physically experienced and embodied by a person.

Imãn brings the perspective of life to embody patience in oneself. 'Ibadah helps this trait to enter into the person as a character trait with practice.

Allah ﷻ opens the different spiritual discoveries with one's engagement of sabr. A daily unexpected encounter of a person with something can reveal the person's degree of sabr, patience.

Omar ra has been depicted as the person who immediately addressed different problems. On the other hand, Abu Bakr ra was narrated to be the person who did not immediately act, but took on a problem with the attitude of calmness and serenity. Omar ra is the symbol of justice, adalah. Yet, Abu Bakr ra as al-siddiq is the symbol of hilm as the mirror image of Rasulullah ﷺ. In this regard, Abu Bakr ra is closest to Rasulullah ﷺ.

It is difficult to remain calm when someone directly accuses another person to one's face. Yet, Abu Bakr ra kept his calmness and serenity [8] (hadith #4896).

In this sense, the level of sabr can indicate one's imãn. Rasulullah ﷺ was the embodiment of sabr with his ﷺ calmness and serenity. Rasulullah ﷺ has the highest level of iman. Abu Bakr ra was his immediate follower and he held the next highest level of iman in the ummah after Rasulullah ﷺ.

Tawakkul, reliance is the fruit of sabr as primarily established with imãn and through the 'ibadah of the person. It is a higher, more positive trait or station that comes to those on a higher level as compared to the level of sabr.

A person of sabr, known as the sãbirìn, can realize and know that something is a test or trial even if it is possibly evil-seeming. He or she shows the attitude of sabr, patience in this situation.

At a higher level, the person of tawakkul sees everything as positive and as a blessing from Allah ﷻ regardless of its outer external cover. At this state, the person is constantly in pleasure as compared to the level of sabr. The level of sabr can sometimes indicate a painful endurance.

Happiness

Eternal happiness can indicate two parts. One can be related to pleasing Allah ﷻ. This is the highest level of happiness that one can achieve. When the person gains nearness and proximity to Allah ﷻ with the guidance of Rasulullah ﷺ, this can fulfill the person in all one's faculties with happiness.

The other happiness can be present due to the bodily satisfactions. This happiness can be present through awareness of one's pleasures through observation, feelings, senses of dwelling, eating, drinking, or through spousal relationships. The happiness gained through these last three fundamental pleasures depend upon continuity and not upon their ending.

The first type of happiness gained from the proximity and pleasing of Allah ﷻ is unarguably clear and does not really need explanation.

The second type of happiness gained through bodily satisfaction can have further elaboration.

When a person knows that he or she is getting the result of one's work as mentioned[90] وَبَشِّرِ الَّذِين آمَنُواْ وَعَمِلُواْ الصَّالِحَاتِ أَنَّ لَهُمْ جَنَّاتٍ, then the person gets more pleasure from the reward. Therefore, a person of آمَنُواْ وَعَمِلُواْ الصَّالِحَاتِ as mentioned in the ayah can maximize the pleasure as the result and reward of one's struggle on the path of Allah ﷻ.

In addition, in Jannah, a person knows that the sustenance is not going to end as the person is not going to die as mentioned خَالِدُونَ. This increases one's pleasure about the ni'mah given by Allah ﷻ. If a person knows the n'imah or the sustenance is limited and therefore going to end, then this worry and concern can make the person uneasy and decrease the pleasure that one derives.

The Qurãn is the nur, light and guidance for the person. Rasulullah ﷺ is the practical guidance. Our emotional states change. We want to be in the company of the virtuous, moral, ethical and pious people in order to receive the benefit of practical guidance. They show us, as role models, how to practice in the realities of life.

Similarly, a good teacher and a good spouse help the person to receive practical guidance as well. There are a lot of times when a person is on the verge of making a decision. Most of the things in life can be hit

90. And give good tidings to those who believe and do righteous deeds that they will have gardens [in Paradise]

or miss if there is no clear guidance from a good friend, a good parent, or a good teacher.

Rasulullah ﷺ embodies the highest level of this practical guidance. Then, other people of Allah ﷻ can follow accordingly. Having a spouse in this life can indicate sharing the common and shared pains, pleasures, and goals in this life. For a Muslim, the spouses share the same goal for the afterlife as well.

In this sense, having a spouse in the akhirah can also indicate this notion of sharing and companionship. It is not only the physical or bodily engagements in spousal relationships but also the notion of sharing and pleasure that follows beyond that level of engagement.

One should remember that the real taste is with marifatullah, knowing and increasing the closeness with Allah ﷻ, and muhabatullah, increasing the love for Allah ﷻ, and i'lm, knowledge related to the path of Allah ﷻ.

When we review the order of the parts in this ayah, the part أَنَّ لَهُمْ جَنَّاتٍ تَجْرِي precedes the previous parts. This can indicate that among human needs, the necessity of dwelling and housing can occur first.

In this regard, the best of residences is the place where there is a green environment with water, a pond, the sea, a river or a lake as mentioned[91] جَنَّاتٍ تَجْرِي مِن تَحْتِهَا الْأَنْهَارُ. In another perspective, the word لأنْهَار can indicate the need for drink being more than the need for food. The need of the person for food as mentioned[92] كُلَّمَا رُزِقُوا مِنْهَا مِن ثَمَرَةٍ follows after the need for drink.

The word ثَمَرَةٍ can indicate fruits in literal translation and also other sustenance items. If the literal translation for ثَمَرَةٍ is taken as 'fruits', one can consider different hikmah as to why other nima'hs are not initially mentioned, such as meat.

In this sense, the word ثَمَرَةٍ can indicate the immediate accessibility of this ni'mah of food as compared to other food items. One doesn't need to cook or even cut most of the fruit. As soon as the person picks it from the tree, we can eat, enjoy, and get energy from it. On the other hand, for example, meat requires slaughtering, slicing, seasoning, and cooking while vegetables can also require cooking and slicing. As a side note, for the people of Allah ﷻ, there is a tradition in Muslim countries

91. Have gardens [in Paradise] beneath which rivers flow.
92. Whenever they are provided with a provision of fruit therefrom,

that they eat dry fruit as a way of immediate access of nutrition to save time and to concentrate on their learning, i'lm, and 'ibadah of Allah ﷻ. For that level of people of Allah ﷻ, spending time cooking can be considered as wasting time and a distraction. Therefore, they quickly satiate their hunger with some dry fruits or food to move on to their real purpose.

One should remember that in the akhirah, all the needs can transform themselves to another level or motivation. In this world, the person needs to have a residence, food, drink, and the continuation of generations through reproduction and company for the person during one's lifetime. Allah ﷻ has placed a motivational pleasure in all cases of needs so that a person can fulfill these needs for existence.

Yet, in the afterlife, the existence of residence, food, or spouse are not due to their end result. Their existence is due to their pleasures. In other words, this life's secondary reason such as pleasure becomes the primary reason in the akhirah.

The Purpose of Spouse

The Need

When we analyze the phrase وَلَهُمْ فِيهَا أَزْوَاجٌ مُّطَهَّرَةٌ, one can focus on the word أَزْوَاجٌ. We have the need for أَزْوَاجٌ in our creation in this world. The only One who does not need أَزْوَاجٌ is Allah ﷻ. This is mentioned[93] سُبْحَانَ الَّذِي خَلَقَ الْأَزْوَاجَ كُلَّهَا مِمَّا تُنبِتُ الْأَرْضُ وَمِنْ أَنفُسِهِمْ وَمِمَّا لَا يَعْلَمُونَ {يس/36}. The expression of سُبْحَانَ in the expression سُبْحَانَ الَّذِي خَلَقَ الْأَزْوَاجَ emphasizes this exception for Allah ﷻ. This is also mentioned as[94] فَاطِرُ السَّمَاوَاتِ وَالْأَرْضِ جَعَلَ لَكُم مِّنْ أَنفُسِكُمْ أَزْوَاجًا وَمِنَ الْأَنْعَامِ أَزْوَاجًا يَذْرَؤُكُمْ فِيهِ لَيْسَ كَمِثْلِهِ شَيْءٌ وَهُوَ السَّمِيعُ الْبَصِيرُ {الشورى/11}. The statement لَيْسَ كَمِثْلِهِ شَيْءٌ وَهُوَ السَّمِيعُ الْبَصِيرُ emphasizes this reality about the Transcendent, Allah ﷻ.

In this sense, accepting our humanness for our need for أَزْوَاجٌ is critical.

93. Exalted is He who created all pairs—from what the earth grows and from themselves and from that which they do not know.

94. [He is] Creator of the heavens and the earth. He has made for you from yourselves, mates, and among the cattle, mates; He multiplies you thereby. There is nothing like unto Him, and He is the Hearing, the Seeing.

Comfort & Solace

One of the purposes of أَزْوَاجً is to have both emotional and physical solace and comfort. This is mentioned[95] وَمِنْ آيَاتِهِ أَنْ خَلَقَ لَكُم مِّنْ أَنفُسِكُمْ أَزْوَاجًا لِّتَسْكُنُوا إِلَيْهَا وَجَعَلَ بَيْنَكُم مَّوَدَّةً وَرَحْمَةً إِنَّ فِي ذَٰلِكَ لَآيَاتٍ لِّقَوْمٍ يَتَفَكَّرُونَ {الروم/21}. One of the examples of this solace and comfort can occur when the spouse can share some incident with the other partner وَإِذْ أَسَرَّ النَّبِيُّ إِلَىٰ بَعْضِ أَزْوَاجِهِ حَدِيثًا as embodied by Rasulullah ﷺ. As Rasulullah ﷺ was the perfect human, he ﷺ showed us how to ideally hold a spousal relationship. In this regard, this example as a side note can show a practical example and guidance for spousal relationships. It is suggested and it is sunnah to discuss with your spouse the daily affairs, incidents, and the things bothering you so as to seek comfort and solace.

This fulfilment of solace and comfort is not gender dependent, but it flows in both directions of mutuality and support is expected from both people in the couple for each other. There is a mutual teaching and advice for each other for the common and shared goals of theirs in this life and in the afterlife.

Common Goals for this Life and the Afterlife

One of the primary expected shared goals in a spousal relationship is to have the same goal for this life and the afterlife. In reality, this primary goal is to help each other to please Allah ﷻ individually and collectively. In this regard, if Allah ﷻ is pleased, then each spouse will be satisfied with his or her own self or ego and at the same time, each will be satisfied with the expectations of each other.

If there is no existence of this shared primary goal, then the relationship will not last and will not be successful. Although this relationship may seem to work in this life, then there will certainly be separation and their true selfishness and egocentrism will be revealed in the afterlife as mentioned[96] إِذَا جَاءَتِ الصَّاخَّةُ {عبس/33} يَوْمَ يَفِرُّ الْمَرْءُ مِنْ أَخِيهِ

---

95. And of His signs is that He created for you from yourselves mates that you may find tranquility in them; and He placed between you affection and mercy. Indeed in that are signs for a people who give thought.

96. 33. But when there comes the Deafening Blast 34. On the Day a man will flee from his brother 35. And his mother and his father 36. And his wife and his children, 37. For every man, that Day, will be a matter adequate for him.

{عبس/34} وَأُمِّهِ وَأَبِيهِ {عبس/35} وَصَاحِبَتِهِ وَبَنِيهِ {عبس/36} لِكُلِّ امْرِئٍ مِّنْهُمْ يَوْمَئِذٍ شَأْنٌ يُغْنِيهِ {عبس/37}

On the other hand, there can be the case of the ones among the couples who support each other and have the same shared evil goal. Then, they end up sharing the same bad outcome together as mentioned

احْشُرُوا الَّذِينَ ظَلَمُوا وَأَزْوَاجَهُمْ وَمَا كَانُوا يَعْبُدُونَ {الصافات/22} [97]

سَيَصْلَى نَارًا ذَاتَ لَهَبٍ {المسد/3} وَامْرَأَتُهُ حَمَّالَةَ الْحَطَبِ {المسد/4}[98]

In this sense, a true spousal relationship requires having the same goal of pleasing Allah ﷻ which equates to being together in this life and in the afterlife as mentioned

وَالَّذِينَ يَقُولُونَ رَبَّنَا هَبْ لَنَا مِنْ أَزْوَاجِنَا وَذُرِّيَّاتِنَا قُرَّةَ أَعْيُنٍ وَاجْعَلْنَا لِلْمُتَّقِينَ إِمَامًا {الفرقان/74}[99]

ادْخُلُوا الْجَنَّةَ أَنتُمْ وَأَزْوَاجُكُمْ تُحْبَرُونَ {الزخرف/70}[100]

In the second scenario, they worked together toward the same goal in this life to please Allah ﷻ, and now they are yearning to be together in the afterlife although one can be higher than the other spiritually. They are helping each other to achieve this shared goal.

Loyalty-Sidq

Yet, the appropriate and chivalrous disposition necessitates sidq, sadaqah, loyalty. You don't forget the favor of any person even if they did a minute favor for you. This trait was embodied by Rasulullah ﷺ.

In this regard, how can a person be so disloyal to her or his partner by not desiring to save the person from Jahannam in the afterlife?

97. [The angels will be ordered], "Gather those who committed wrong, their kinds, and what they used to worship
98. 3. He will [enter to] burn in a Fire of [blazing] flame 4. And his wife [as well]—the carrier of firewood.
99. And those who say, "Our Lord, grant us from among our wives and offspring comfort to our eyes and make us an example for the righteous."
100. Enter Paradise, you and your kinds, delighted."

Even any wicked person who has a little bit of good in his or her heart would not desire to have one's partner and friend be punished in fire.

In this regard, the primary reason for divorce is due to not having or understanding this common and shared goal in this life and in the afterlife.

Divorces occur due to blaming and being angry with one's partner for different reasons. The couples lacking the understanding of this blessed primary goal may concoct different reasons to blame each other. These blames can be related to issues of children, finances, individual character traits, expectations, etc.

A good spouse can constantly ask the other partner, "How can I help you today so that you can please Allah ﷻ? How can I help you today with all of the needs of the children and house so that you can do some khalwah, spending time with Allah ﷻ without much or any distraction?"

In this type of engagement, if Allah ﷻ is pleased with each spouse, then Allah ﷻ can put barakah, blessing in their engagements and family relationships.

Appreciation

One can ask this question, "Why do we see pious or religious-seeming couples also experiencing divorce?"

One should understand that loyalty, sidq requires patience, sabr and constant effort of cleaning the hearts towards each other and not making su-I zann, assuming bad about each other. Even a small favor from another person requires a type of sidq and loyalty to this person. This is not only about spousal relationship. This is true in 'abd, makhluq, and Khaliq, Allah SWT relationships, parent and child relationships, student and teacher relationships, friend relationships, and even person and object relationships. It is interpreted that Rasulullah ﷺ, al-Habib ﷺ named his ﷺ personal items, such as his hairbrush, in order to show appreciation to them.

In our human relationships, we show our primary appreciation to Allah ﷻ for giving us that bounty. At the same time, we show our appreciation toward that person for being the lofty means of this benefit for us as truly and essentially supplied by Allah SWT.

When this point is missed, mere religiosity or piety without embodiment is not carried out. The true result of 'ibadah develops one's character to be patient in fighting against evil as mentioned[101] اتْلُ مَا أُوحِيَ إِلَيْكَ مِنَ الْكِتَابِ وَأَقِمِ الصَّلَاةَ إِنَّ الصَّلَاةَ تَنْهَى عَنِ الْفَحْشَاءِ وَالْمُنكَرِ وَلَذِكْرُ اللَّهِ أَكْبَرُ وَاللَّهُ يَعْلَمُ مَا تَصْنَعُونَ {العنكبوت/45}

In the scenario in which one spouse may not truly understand the embodiment of a common shared goal to please Allah , then the one who understands needs to practice and embody patience. In this sense, Allah does not mention divorce, but being patient with one's spouse and overlooking his or her faults as mentioned[102] يَا أَيُّهَا الَّذِينَ آمَنُوا إِنَّ مِنْ أَزْوَاجِكُمْ وَأَوْلَادِكُمْ عَدُوًّا لَّكُمْ فَاحْذَرُوهُمْ وَإِن تَعْفُوا وَتَصْفَحُوا وَتَغْفِرُوا فَإِنَّ اللَّهَ غَفُورٌ رَّحِيمٌ {التغابن/14}

Anything that distracts the person from pleasing Allah can be referred to as عَدُوًّا لَّكُمْ. If this is a person who is a believer, especially a spouse or children, then the person should try to distance himself or herself from the evil as mentioned فَاحْذَرُوهُمْ and embody patience and overlook his or her mistakes as mentioned with وَإِن تَعْفُوا وَتَصْفَحُوا وَتَغْفِرُو. This disposition can lead the person to be among those who are forgiven by Allah as mentioned فَإِنَّ اللَّهَ غَفُورٌ رَّحِيمٌ {التغابن/14}.

One should pay attention to that fact that loyalty and sidq require on to have patience with people, especially with family. Allah does not mention divorce as a solution to the evil renderings of affiliates, but rather advises وَإِن تَعْفُوا وَتَصْفَحُوا وَتَغْفِرُوا.

Valuation System

وَبَشِّرِ الَّذِين آمَنُواْ وَعَمِلُواْ الصَّالِحَاتِ أَنَّ لَهُمْ جَنَّاتٍ تَجْرِي مِن تَحْتِهَا الأَنْهَارُ كُلَّمَا رُزِقُواْ مِنْهَا مِن ثَمَرَةٍ رِّزْقاً قَالُواْ هَذَا الَّذِي رُزِقْنَا مِن قَبْلُ وَأُتُواْ بِهِ مُتَشَابِهاً وَلَهُمْ فِيهَا أَزْوَاجٌ مُّطَهَّرَةٌ وَهُمْ فِيهَا خَالِدُونَ {البقرة/25}[103]

101. Recite, [O Muhammad], what has been revealed to you of the Book and establish prayer. Indeed, prayer prohibits immorality and wrongdoing, and the remembrance of Allah is greater. And Allah knows that which you do.

102. O you who have believed, indeed, among your wives and your children are enemies to you, so beware of them. But if you pardon and overlook and forgive—then indeed, Allah is Forgiving and Merciful.

103. And give good tidings to those who believe and do righteous deeds that they will have gardens [in Paradise] beneath which rivers flow. Whenever they are provided with a provision of fruit therefrom, they will say, "This is what we were provided with before." And it is given to them in likeness. And they will have therein purified spouses, and they will abide therein eternally.

قُلْ أَؤُنَبِّئُكُم بِخَيْرٍ مِّن ذَٰلِكُمْ لِلَّذِينَ اتَّقَوْا عِندَ رَبِّهِمْ جَنَّاتٌ تَجْرِي مِن تَحْتِهَا الأَنْهَارُ خَالِدِينَ فِيهَا وَأَزْوَاجٌ مُّطَهَّرَةٌ وَرِضْوَانٌ مِّنَ اللهِ وَاللهُ بَصِيرٌ بِالْعِبَادِ {آل عمران/14}[104]

وَالَّذِينَ آمَنُواْ وَعَمِلُواْ الصَّالِحَاتِ سَنُدْخِلُهُمْ جَنَّاتٍ تَجْرِي مِن تَحْتِهَا الأَنْهَارُ خَالِدِينَ فِيهَا أَبَدًا لَّهُمْ فِيهَا أَزْوَاجٌ مُّطَهَّرَةٌ وَنُدْخِلُهُمْ ظِلاًّ ظَلِيلاً {النساء/57}[105]

It is very critical to analyze the spousal relationships through the valuation system of the Qurãn and the sunnah of Rasulullah ﷺ. Especially, this is very critical when different ideas and philosophies are constantly flowing through changing moral, ethical, and social value systems. Especially, Western dominance of financial hegemony causes the masses to conform to the Western value system. The supposition is: 'If their financial system is better than ours, then their moral, ethical, and social value system is also better than ours. So, we should also adapt this value system.'

As it is important to analyze the verses of the Qurãn through the lens of their opposite implied meanings, it is also important to analyze the critical expression أَزْوَاجٌ مُّطَهَّرَةٌ in the above verses.

The first implied meaning is that the spouses in this life are not مُّطَهَّرَةٌ. When one reviews the tafãsir about the interpretation of this word within its context [3], one can find the interpretations of both physical and spiritual uncleanliness.

In this case, it can be important to focus on the context of this word مُّطَهَّرَةٌ within the context of spiritual uncleanliness which is also mentioned as a bad character trait or personality.

When we review the terms such as 'bad character' or 'bad personality', this can generally imply choice in the attitudes of people. This notion of choice forming the attitude or character comes after the deliberate decision making of a person. All of a person's decisions are made according to a value system.

104. Say, "Shall I inform you of [something] better than that? For those who fear Allah ﷻ will be gardens in the presence of their Lord beneath which rivers flow, wherein they abide eternally, and purified spouses and approval from Allah ﷻ. And Allah ﷻ is Seeing of [His] servants

105. But those who believe and do righteous deeds—We will admit them to gardens beneath which rivers flow, wherein they abide forever. For them therein are purified spouses, and We will admit them to deepening shade.

Regardless of whether or not a person accepts or realizes it, every individual does have a personalized value system. This value system can be formed implicitly or explicitly and intentionally or unintentionally.

Every person has an individualized value system. This value system can change over the lifespan of a person. The amount of change can increase from childhood until senility.

If there is a constant abundance of change in one's valuation system, some people can view this as negatively as immaturity. Conversely, some people can view this positively as open-mindedness. If there is not much change in one's valuation system, some people can view this as stubbornness or narrow mindedness as a negative trait. Conversely, some people can view this as an established trait or personality with maturity as evidence of a positive character.

All of the above points signal and emphasize the importance of having a set and proper valuation system by choice and with a proper intention. If a personal valuation system is inevitable, then this shows that a person should make every effort to choose and follow a valuation system according to one's goal and purpose in life.

Coming back to our original point about the word مُطَهَّرَةٌ, almost all of the conflicts that occur between couples are due to this blurred and unidentified valuation system.

A Muslim man constantly confused about his purpose and goal in life will definitely have confusion in his valuation system.

A Muslim woman constantly confused about her purpose and goal in life will definitely have confusion in her valuation system.

This confusion in their valuation systems will be displayed in practical cases when each person is on the verge of making decisions. These confused stances will label each of them or each of their characters or attitudes to be evil, wicked, and malicious or to be good and acceptable.

To give some practical examples, backbiting is a very critical sin and it can be worse than adultery [9] as mentioned by Rasulullah ﷺ. Yet, if the culture or valuation system endorses backbiting in professional and social environments in meetings, gatherings, and on social media, then a Muslim confused in his or her valuation system will follow them contrary to his or her true goal and purpose and what he or she claims to follow.

Another example can be with the term 'abuse'. If a term such as 'abuse' is increasingly popularized in liberal systems aiming to remove all types of structure, hierarchy, and order indicating an assumed arrogance of self-sufficiency, then a confused Muslim will borrow these terms from a value system belonging to others and use it in marital and family relationships. He or she will follow them although contrary to his or her true goal and purpose and what he or she claims to follow.

There is nothing wrong with borrowing terms from different valuation systems. Islam is clearly against all forms of abuse.

Yet, a follower without any set valuation system, in the absence of constantly checking the bugs in these borrowed terms, will slowly erode the content of his or her original valuation system representing his or her true goal and purpose.

I think it is very important to openly discuss, what we mean by the terms 'abuse', 'bullying', 'freedom', 'rights', etc. These all seem to be hashtags for the beginning of a good cause in their externality. Yet, they need to be evaluated within the valuation system of the individual representing his or her goal and purpose in life.

For example, a sign of an abuser according to modern psychology, counseling, and social work is that if there is problem between individuals such as between couples, then if the abuser buys the other person a gift after the abuse is over, then this is one of the signs and proofs that there is an abuse.

On the other hand, in our concept of relationships transferred from our embedded Islamic cultures, we make mistakes and it is important to ask forgiveness and to buy gifts for people if we think that we have broken their hearts.

In the prior case, as soon as the person buys a gift, the instruction from the modern social worker, psychologist, or counselor is that this is evidence of abuse. Therefore, the person should and must end the relationship.

In the latter case of a Muslim valuation system, we forgive each other and move on. We receive the gift as something positive that expresses the regret of the other party. We are not advised to assume evil thoughts or feelings or to perceive gift giving as another form of abuse.

It is true that everything has a context. A gift can be a form of abuse in some contexts. Yet, I think generalizing that a gift is a sign of abuse is a very evil approach in modern counseling. These approaches promote conflict, separation, selfishness, arrogance, and self-sufficiency.

The other case promotes empathy, forgiveness, humbleness, and dependence on Allah ﷻ.

One can lead to kufr, lack of appreciation, constant complaining, unhappiness, misery, anxiety, fear, and stress.

The other can lead to imãn, appreciation, happiness, calmness, wisdom, and tranquility.

One leads to the displeasure of Allah ﷻ and the most disliked halal option is divorce [6][106].

The other leads to the pleasure of Allah ﷻ keeping the unity, jam'ah and collectiveness for a good cause, for the family, and for the society at large.

Yet, the word مُطَهَّرَة implies and normalizes the existence of these problems in spousal relationships in this world. With the Fadl and Rahmah of Allah ﷻ, couples will have a perfect relationship with full satisfaction and happiness in Jannah.

Knowing and having this expectation of مُطَهَّرَة in Jannah can give extra stamina and patience to overlook the problems in this world especially when things become ugly and messy in spousal relationships. May Allah ﷻ protect us from the trials of spouses, children, and family, Amìn!

The Concern for Ending & Locating Different Emotions

When a person is engaged with a bounty, pleasure, or happiness, one of the feelings that decreases the effect of this happiness is worry and concern about its ending. The bargaining of children desiring to play more than their timed period, and the concern of humans to live longer and not die can be some of the examples of these intrinsic desires of humans.

According to the one approach [5], the desire of humans to not die or their desire for never-ending pleasures are intrinsic emotions given by Allah ﷻ to the people for a purpose. This purpose is to first detect and diagnose this desire and then to channel it to the correct means.

The emphasis of وَهُمْ فِيهَا خَالِدُونَ in different forms in the Qurãn can imply the removal of this pain causing anxiety, worry, and concern for

106. Book 10, Hadith 2096

the person. When the person knows that the pleasure and happiness that he or she is experiencing is not going to end, then the quality and quantity of pleasure is amplified and boosted up.

The feeling of the desire is given to humans by Allah ﷻ so that they can use it as a guidance to find a place where the call for this feeling can be satisfied. As one tracks the pathway of this feeling, then it leads the person to the result of the necessity and existence of an endless afterlife. Then, the person can rationalize and fulfill the requirements for being in the position of living an endless life in Jannah.

In this regard, all the emotions and desires are given for a purpose so that they can be placed in their appropriate positions [6] [7]. One should really first know oneself. Knowing oneself requires detecting all of these emotions individually, discretely, and separately. Then, it is important to be able to call them by certain names as the ayah can indicate. The next step is understanding and analyzing them with their purposes as assigned by Allah ﷻ in the person. After all of that, it is important to engage oneself constantly in the struggle of keeping the balance of all of these emotions leading to different mental and emotional states with balance. Yet, the struggle of the person to keep the balance can also be named the trials and tests of life as well.

We can take the example of anger.

Anger is not, by its mere existence, a disease in a person. Allah ﷻ made this feeling present so that a person can feel a driving force and be motivated to do something against an injustice. On the other hand, it is given by Allah ﷻ in order to reveal a person's reality as a test or trial if he or she can establish balance in the proper usage of this feeling. Anger can lead to oppression, abuse, and injustice. Yet, positive anger can lead to doing something and standing against injustices and establishing structure.

One can refer to this appropriate, balanced perspective as istiqamah, continuity of balance. Another can call this al-haqq, the truth and reality. Another can define this as the correct fulfillment of being khalifah, of Allah ﷻ on the earth.

Similarly, one can extend a similar approach for other feelings, emotions, or states. These can be in human terms such as arrogance, jealousy, the desire for endless pleasure or life, etc.

Arrogance is the name of a negative emotional state that can lead the person to claim something that he or she does not possess. This is a negative state of destruction. This especially becomes very destructive if one claims it in his or her relationship with Allah ﷻ. Yet, another positive term is having an identity and self as the creation and 'abd of Allah ﷻ. In this regard, the arrogance transforms into the pride of being of 'abd of Allah ﷻ. Then, this embodiment of a person as the 'abdullah elevates the person above all fears, anxieties, and worries. It places the person in the states of confidence, tawakkul, taslim, and reliance on Allah ﷻ and independent of all creation. This is not the negative state of arrogance, but the positive state of gina, not being dependent on anything except Allah ﷻ.

Jealousy is the negative state of a desire for others to lose what they have. The jealous person hates others and destroys himself or herself with this destruction as mentioned by al-Habib ﷺ (4903) [8]. Yet, one can transform this into a feeling of gibta for some specific lofty bounties. In this case, one can ask Allah ﷻ to have this bounty for himself or herself and yet at the same time, ask Allah ﷻ to increase his or her brother in that specific bounty more than before. This lofty bounty can be acquirement of knowledge, or any means that can lead the person to a good action to please Allah ﷻ.

Jannah and Fadl & Rahmah of Allah ﷻ

When we analyze the statement[107] وَبَشِّرِ الَّذِينَ آمَنُواْ وَعَمِلُواْ الصَّالِحَاتِ أَنَّ لَهُمْ جَنَّاتٍ تَجْرِي مِن تَحْتِهَا الأَنْهَارُ, the phrase بَشِّرِ can indicate that the result of Jannah is not due to the acquisition or right of the person, but rather it is due to the Fadl and Rahmah of Allah .ﷻ A deserved right is not expressed with the word بَشِّر, tabshìr. If it is a right, then it is expressed as, 'your right is given to you'. Yet, when a person wins a lottery in our worldly means, it is not the right of the person.

In our lives, we try to attract the Fadl and Rahmah of Allah ﷻ with our deeds and intentions with the primary recognition of Allah ﷻ with imãn. Then, it is the Fadl and Rahmah of Allah ﷻ that we try to be from the ones as mentioned[108] وَبَشِّرِ الَّذِين آمَنُواْ وَعَمِلُواْ الصَّالِحَاتِ.

In that sense, going to Jannah is not a right but a privilege given by Allah ﷻ as a Fadl and Rahmah. There are a lot of narratives and stories

107. And give good tidings to those who believe and do righteous deeds that they will have gardens [in Paradise] beneath which rivers flow.
108. And give good tidings to those who believe and do righteous deeds

of the people of piety that indicate that they were given the glad tidings of Jannah with their attraction of the Fadl and Rahmah of Allah ﷻ due to a simple-looking deed and not due to their lives filled with piety.

Our goal in our lives is to involve ourselves as much as possible with the deeds of ‘ibadah and amalu salih with ikhlas to please Allah ﷻ so that we can have the Rahmah and Fadl of Allah ﷻ.

We don’t trust in our actions, deeds, or ‘ibadah but we do trust in the Mercy, Rahmah, and Fadl of Allah ﷻ.

Another interesting point in وَبَشِّرِ الَّذِين آمَنُوا وَعَمِلُوا الصَّالِحَاتِ is related with the responsibility and position of Rasulullah ﷺ with risalah, prophethood. The siga, form بَشِّرِ is in amr, order form. This indicates that Rasulullah ﷺ is not in the position of giving glad tidings and good news about the future life of a person in the afterlife. Rasulullah ﷺ cannot guarantee Jannah or decide for the aqibah, ending of a person. Allah ﷻ is the Ultimate Knower and Decision Maker of everyone’s ending.

The responsibility of Rasulullah ﷺ is tabligh, inviting people to Allah ﷻ. In this perspective, the word بَشِّرِ can indicate the expected method of tabligh for Rasulullah ﷺ and for us. This should be with the engagements of بَشِّرِ giving glad tidings, encouragement, love, and positive reinforcement and inspiration to people. Yes, there is the inzãr, warning and fear perspective of tabligh. Yet, one of the names of Rasulullah is al-bashìr, the one who gives glad tidings. This can be our dominant method of engagement with people. Rasulullah ﷺ is rahmatan lil alamin, mercy for all. We should study and adapt all the traits of Rasulullah ﷺ as al-bashìr in all perspectives of our lives, inshAllah.

When one compares the two expressions in the beginning of the surãh as[109] الَّذِينَ يُؤْمِنُونَ بِالْغَيْبِ وَيُقِيمُونَ الصَّلَاةَ وَمِمَّا رَزَقْنَاهُمْ يُنفِقُونَ {البقرة/3} and وَبَشِّرِ الَّذِين آمَنُوا وَعَمِلُوا الصَّالِحَاتِ, there is a difference in the tenses between يُؤْمِنُونَ and آمَنُوا. The first one يُؤْمِنُونَ is in mudãri, present and future tenses for encouragement and the second one آمَنُوا is in past form to indicate that the results of the achievements are given at the end. In other words, one receives the result of their past and completed engagements.

In the expression وَبَشِّرِ الَّذِين آمَنُوا وَعَمِلُوا الصَّالِحَاتِ, the conjunction وَ indicates togetherness with the cited item. At another perspective آمَنُوا indicates the primary requirement and عَمِلُوا الصَّالِحَاتِ indicate the

109. Who believe in the unseen, establish prayer, and spend out of what We have provided for them,

secondary requirement that the primary requirement necessitates. In simple logic, this can be indicated as

A (primary) ⟶ B (secondary) — A necessitates and requires B

B (secondary) A (primary) — B does not necessarily necessitate A

In other words, if someone has imãn, it is expected that this person will and should display good actions, amalu salìh. Iman necessitates, requires, and embodies in the person the display of good, ethical, and moral actions. On the other hand, some people can display outwardly good, ethical, and moral actions but this does not necessarily necessitate the existence of imãn. It is possible but not required.

A person of kufr can engage with moral and ethical actions in order to leave a legacy of remembrance of good reputation, fame, and other motivating factors as social activists engage themselves. A person of imãn engages himself or herself with good actions to please Allah ﷻ regardless of whether or not people see or know about it. In fact, a person of imãn with ikhlas wants his or her actions not to be known by people but only to be known by Allah ﷻ in order to stress and underline the intention of his or her engagements. This is only and solely to please Allah ﷻ. Allahumma J'alna Minhum اللهمَّ جَعَلنَا مِنهُم.

In many places of the Qurãn, the expression وَعَمِلُواْ الصَّالِحَاتِ is a generally repeated term. On most occasions, this expression وَعَمِلُواْ الصَّالِحَاتِ can indicate a general term of virtuous, ethical, and moral deeds and actions. According to one perspective, the reason is that most of the time the ethical action and morality are known and agreed upon in a society through the transferred knowledge and experience from one generation to another. This knowledge and experience can be due to the prior scriptures sent by Allah ﷻ and also due to the intrinsic, natural fitrah qualities of a human being.

In another perspective, the expression وَعَمِلُواْ الصَّالِحَاتِ can be the general name of previously mentioned actions such as[110] وَيُقِيمُونَ الصَّلَاةَ وَمِمَّا رَزَقْنَاهُمْ يُنفِقُونَ {البقرة/3}.

When we analyze the expression[111] أَنَّ لَهُمْ جَنَّاتٍ تَجْرِي مِن تَحْتِهَا الأَنْهَارُ, there is the ta'kid, emphasis on the word أَنَّ. Sometimes, when a person

110. Who believe in the unseen, establish prayer, and spend out of what We have provided for them,

111. that they will have gardens [in Paradise] beneath which rivers flow.

is describing something that is impossible and difficult to immediately believe and grasp, he or she may feel the need to take an oath to emphasize its truth and reality in order to remove any possible doubts from people's minds. Similarly, the word أَنَّ shows this pledge and assurance about the existence of Jannah as having been prepared marvelously for the believers. Allahumma Ja'alna minhum. Amìn.

The word لَهُمْ is forwarded to the front line to emphasize the specific particularity and ownership of Jannah. In other words, لَهُمْ could have been present as[112] .أَنَّ لَهُمْ جَنَّاتٍ تَجْرِي مِن تَحْتِهَا الْأَنْهَارُ Yet, it is promoted to the front line to emphasize that

Jannah is specifically prepared for believers. Believers are not going to a place that has already been used by others in the past. It is fresh, new, and only and solely prepared for the people of imãn. One can remember the experience of living in a newly and freshly built house as compared to a used house with its problems, smells, and repairs.

Jannah is owned by the believers, and it is not a rental. In other words, owning something gives someone more pleasure, comfort, and peace of mind than renting or leasing it. The feeling of owning in itself has its own pleasure.

The word جَنَّاتٍ can indicate the awesome and marvelous features of Jannah by being in the form of nakra. When it is not specified with the m'arifah of alif and lãm, then this nakra form can indicate different levels of Jannah with different levels of astonishments, features, and pleasures.

Once when analyzes the expression تَجْرِي مِن تَحْتِهَا الأَنْهَارُ, one can realize the word تَجْرِي is used to indicate the effect of flowing water on human psychology leading to tranquility, calmness, pleasure, and happiness. The effect of water on human psychology is indicated in some of the recent fieldworks as well [8]. The word تَجْرِي especially indicates the flowing water as compared to stagnant water without any motion, sound, and visual change.

In another analysis, the expression مِن تَحْتِهَا الأَنْهَارُ, can indicate the benefits of different types of water such as well water coming from under the ground and spring water flowing from mountains as indicated with تَجْرِي مِن تَحْتِهَا الأَنْهَار. The minerals included in water content can increase its benefits as an essential need for humans. One can find these essential

112. that they will have gardens [in Paradise] beneath which rivers flow.

benefits in water especially coming naturally from well and spring water unlike filtered waters [10].

The plural form of الأَنْهَارُ can indicate different lines of flowing water. In this sense, this can increase the pleasure of scenery for a person whose dwelling is in close vicinity to these water sources. Besides its visual pleasures, different sounds of the flowing water can be orchestrated with multiple arches of flowing water at different speeds. A multitude of water sources can also give more accessibility to different water sources to show abundance, ease, and peace of mind.

When we analyze the expression كُلَّمَا رُزِقُواْ مِنْهَا مِن ثَمَرَةٍ رِّزْقاً, the word كُلَّمَا can indicate the continuity of sustenance without any end. The word رُزِقُواْ in the majhul, passive, form can indicate that the food is served to the dwellers of Jannah and that there is no difficulty in working, finding, earning for it, preparing, or serving the food. The expression مِنْهَا مِن ثَمَرَةٍ is used instead of مِن ثَمَرَتِهَا in order to indicate that everything in Jannah is sustenance, ثَمَرَةٍ, for its dwellers. The word رِّزْقاً in the nakrah form in the expression مِن ثَمَرَةٍ رِّزْقاً clarifies that the engagement of the dwellers of Jannah with sustenance or food is not due to need but it is due to pleasure.

When one analyzes the ayah[113] قَالُواْ هَذَا الَّذِي رُزِقْنَا مِن قَبْلُ وَأُتُواْ بِهِ مُتَشَابِهاً وَلَهُمْ فِيهَا أَزْوَاجٌ مُّطَهَّرَةٌ وَهُمْ فِيهَا خَالِدُونَ {البقرة/25} the word, فِيهَا is repeated in وَلَهُمْ فِيهَا أَزْوَاجٌ مُّطَهَّرَةٌ وَهُمْ فِيهَا خَالِدُونَ. The repetition of this word فِيهَا can indicate and underlines that there are certain special bounties of Allah ﷻ only given in Jannah. Some of them can be فِيهَا خَالِدُونَ that there is no death. There is endless life. Although in this world, the person can have the desire to live an endless life, this is truly not possible in this life. This is only possible in Jannah.

In that sense, there is an emphasis with فِيهَاthat there are unique bounties in Jannah only special to Jannah compared to مُتَشَابِهاً and that some of the bounties can remind the person of prior bounties given in this world. Both can bring different types of pleasures, satisfaction, and happiness. Both unique ones and the ones similar to this life can maximize joy at different levels.

In this sense, sometimes, when something is fully new, unexpected, and unusual, a person can express some type of discomfort or fear with

113. They will say, "This is what we were provided with before." And it is given to them in likeness. And they will have therein purified spouses, and they will abide therein eternally.

the word 'creepy' or 'strange' in American English colloquial language. In this sense, these words can imply something not previously visited, seen, or encountered; unfamiliar or alien, unusual or surprising in a way that is unsettling or hard to understand unaccustomed to or unfamiliar with causing an unpleasant feeling of fear or unease [2] On the other hand, something fully the same as routine can imply something to be monotonous, boring, unstimulating dull, tedious, and repetitious; lacking in variety and interest [2]

One can realize the optimization of the pleasures in Jannah by bringing in both perspectives. This is another miracle of the Qurãn found in one ayah by analyzing two words in their implied meanings, SubhanAllah!

Emotional Memories

When we analyze the expression قَالُواْ هَٰذَا الَّذِي رُزِقْنَا مِن قَبْلُ, one can remember the pleasure of remembering and recollecting memories. There are different theories on memories, recollection of the past experience in the field of cognitive science.

In this case, remembering a pleasure in the past and knowing it will exist in the future can give pleasure, happiness, and comfort for the psychology of the person. The person knows that a pleasure that he or she has in this world will continue in the afterlife, and is not going to end. This feeling and knowledge can in itself give the person hope, motivation, and encouragement to work.

Humans especially are motivated when they know what they will get at the end of their work. If the result is something so high that they cannot imagine it, then this in itself can cause problems in the motivation of the person. Most humans would like to have access to the immediate result of their work either in their imaginations, minds, or some type of experience. Humans are not patient, but they are hasty as mentioned[114] خُلِقَ الْإِنسَانُ مِنْ عَجَلٍ سَأُرِيكُمْ آيَاتِي فَلَا تَسْتَعْجِلُونِ {الأنبياء/37}.

There are a lot of stories among people that allude to this reality. One of them is related in the tale of a shepherd being invited to a feast at a king's or sultan's palace. Among hundreds of different foods available at the feast, the shepherd was not happy and did not feel that he was at a

114. Man was created of haste. I will show you My signs, so do not impatiently urge Me.

feast. The shepherd was looking for his most valued food that he used to enjoy on rare occasions. This was bread crunches in fresh milk.

Similarly, the ayah can indicate our built-up and expected engagements of pleasure in this world to be carried on to the next world as mentioned with the قَالُواْ هَذَا الَّذِي رُزِقْنَا مِن قَبْلُ وَأُتُواْ بِهِ مُتَشَابِهاً. This is to motivate the person in this life for the expected outcomes in the afterlife.

At another level, when some people die today, people get together to remember this person by sharing some memories. This can be known in popular culture as 'the remembering or recollection of a deceased person, especially one who was popular or respected' [2]. In this sense, the word قَالُواْ can indicate this type of collective remembrance of the shared experiences and emotional memories.

In other words, when emotional memories are remembered by the individual, then it has an effect on the person. When the same shared emotional memories are remembered and commemorated collectively as mentioned with قَالُواْ, then it can have some amplified effects leading to further pleasure, satisfaction, and happiness.

The word مُتَشَابِهاً in the phrase قَالُواْ هَذَا الَّذِي رُزِقْنَا مِن قَبْلُ وَأُتُواْ بِهِ مُتَشَابِهاً can indicate two perspectives as well.

The first one is that there can be pleasure in habits. When a person continues his or her daily habit, there is an embedded pleasure in this habit. There is the case of the negative and boring perspective of routines as well. Yet, the habits such as going to work daily, working out, daily readings, and other scheduled regular practices can make a person happy. Similarly, the word مُتَشَابِهاً can indicate the pleasure in the routines.

The second one is that مُتَشَابِهاً can indicate that what will be given in the afterlife will not be exactly the same as what was experienced in the world. This can resolve the issues about the negative side of routines. Although these routines may look alike, they will be different and changing to increase the pleasure of the person with these bounties given by Allah ﷻ.

[26-27][115]

إِنَّ اللهَ لاَ يَسْتَحْيِي أَن يَضْرِبَ مَثَلاً مَّا بَعُوضَةً فَمَا فَوْقَهَا فَأَمَّا الَّذِينَ آمَنُواْ فَيَعْلَمُونَ
أَنَّهُ الْحَقُّ مِن رَّبِّهِمْ وَأَمَّا الَّذِينَ كَفَرُواْ فَيَقُولُونَ مَاذَا أَرَادَ اللهُ بِهَذَا مَثَلاً يُضِلُّ بِهِ كَثِيراً
وَيَهْدِي بِهِ كَثِيراً وَمَا يُضِلُّ بِهِ إِلاَّ الْفَاسِقِينَ {البقرة/26} الَّذِينَ يَنقُضُونَ عَهْدَ اللهِ مِن بَعْدِ
مِيثَاقِهِ وَيَقْطَعُونَ مَا أَمَرَ اللهُ بِهِ أَن يُوصَلَ وَيُفْسِدُونَ فِي الأَرْضِ أُولَئِكَ هُمُ الْخَاسِرُونَ
{البقرة/27}

Manifestations and Reflections of Names and Attributes of Allah ﷻ

The expression إِنَّ اللهَ لاَ يَسْتَحْيِي can indicate human problems in the true tawhid of Allah ﷻ. The manifestation of Will-Iradah, Power-Qudrah, and Knowledge-I'lm of Allah ﷻ is Infinite. Humans may get some type of clue about the different Names and Attributes of Allah ﷻ through the A'fāl, the Manifested Divine Actions of Allah ﷻ. These are all manifestations or reflections. They cannot be replaced with the Real. Yet, one should remember that the manifestation of these af'āl can give a person a clue about ma'rifatullah (true knowledge about Allah ﷻ).

Yet, one should realize the manifestation of different Names and Attributes of Allah ﷻ constantly, in similar and different places, contexts, and beings. Looking at only one Attribute and Name of Allah ﷻ in only one manifestation and trying to approximate one's understanding about Allah ﷻ through only one Name and Attribute cannot be the best way to approach the true ma'rifah of Allah ﷻ. One can love one Name and Attribute of Allah ﷻ a lot. Especially, one can realize the manifestation of one Name and Attribute of Allah ﷻ in particular in the spiritual travel (sulûq) of a person. At this state (maqām), the spiritual traveler can be overwhelmed with this One Name and Attribute of Allah ﷻ. When this state is over, then the traveler comes to the reality of knowing and realizing other Names and Attributes of Allah ﷻ.

This shows that one can approximate to ma'rifatullah by studying and experiencing different Names and Attributes of Allah ﷻ. The effort of a wholistic and comprehensive approach in understanding different

115. 26. Indeed, Allah ﷻ is not timid to present an example—that of a mosquito or what is smaller than it. And those who have believed know that it is the truth from their Lord. But as for those who disbelieve, they say, "What did Allah ﷻ intend by this as an example?" He misleads many thereby and guides many thereby. And He misleads not except the defiantly disobedient, 27. Who break the covenant of Allah after contracting it and sever that which Allah ﷻ has ordered to be joined and cause corruption on earth. It is those who are the losers.

Names and Attributes of Allah ﷻ is extremely important. This can lead to true tawhid and yaqìn in the imãn of a person. Therefore, Rasulullah ﷺ encourages us to know and to memorize the 99 Names of Allah ﷻ in the tradition. There are more Names of Allah ﷻ than the 99 Names. The Names of Allah ﷻ are countless as mentioned in different texts. Yet, the compilation of 99 Names as a collective unit is a famous tradition encouraged by Rasulullah ﷺ and mentioned in the hadith [2] (6597) and [5] (2677). This can be the initial stage and training for Muslims to struggle constantly for the true m'arifah of Allah ﷻ leading to true imãn with yaqìn.

Similarly, humans may get some type of clue about different Names and Attributes of Allah ﷻ through the Manifested Words-Kalãm of Allah ﷻ. In this regard, the Qurãn, Injìl, Tawrah, and others are all Kalãm of Allah ﷻ sent to humans. These Divine Kãlam indicate and explain to us different Names and Attributes of Allah ﷻ. One should remember that the manifestation of these Kalãm can give a person some understanding about ma'rifatullah (true knowledge about Allah ﷻ). These are all manifestations or reflections in our realm. They cannot replace the Real.

One can realize the manifestation of different Names and Attributes of Allah ﷻ constantly, in similar and different places, contexts, and descriptions as mentioned in the Qurãn. Looking at only one ãyah or surãh or through only one manifestation and trying to approximate one's understanding about Allah ﷻ through only one Name and Attribute cannot be the best way to approach true ma'rifah.

One can love one sûrah or ayah a lot. This is normal and virtuous. The effort of a wholistic and comprehensive approach to understanding the entire Qurãn is extremely important. This can lead to true tawhid and yaqìn in imãn in a person. Therefore, Rasulullah ﷺ encourages us to know and memorize certain sûrahs and ayahs. For example, Sûrahs al- Fatiha, al-Yãsin, al-Mulk, al-Kahf, al-Sajdah, al-Dukhan, al-Waqi'ah, al-Ikhlas, al-Falaq, and al-Nãs are some of them. Ayatal Kursi, Ãmana Rasulu in Sûrah Baqara, and the last ayahs of Sûrah Hashr are some other examples. This can be the initial stage and training for Muslims to struggle constantly for the true m'arifah of Allah ﷻ leading to true imãn with yaqìn by approaching the Qurãn fully, and wholistically.

One should remember that all these Af'ãl and Kalãm are manifestations or reflections. They cannot be replace the Real. These are all manifestation or reflections in different realms-a'lam. A'lam

Shadadah and A'lam Malakût are different a'lams and they have different manifestations.

Yet, one should differentiate all of these manifestations and reflections in different realms or a'lam from the Real, Dhãt of Allah ﷻ.

Embodiment of Salah

One should remember that everything in their realm of Malakût is noble. In their interaction on the plane of Shadadah, they have the external skin of evil, good, or neutral. The causes in the realm of Shadadah are covers to protect one's imãn so that they don't lose adab with Allah ﷻ in terms of attributing blame and evil to Allah ﷻ, astagfirullah, SubhanAllahul Azìm.

The A'zamah, Nobility and Highness of Allah ﷻ requires the causalities to act as a cover in the executions in this world hiding the realities behind them. The Wahdaniyyah, Oneness of Allah ﷻ indicates control and surrounding of everything beyond the causalities. One of the Names of Allah ﷻ is Musabbabul Asbab, the Real Cause behind all apparent causes.

Therefore, we need to constantly remember the A'zamah of Allah ﷻ with perfection in our ruku' and with perfection as Subhana Rabbiya al-Azìm سبحان ربي العظيم.

At a higher level, one should remember that Allah ﷻ is higher than all of the human value systems of construction. Admitting this reality and always negating the problematic issues and replacing them further than the dhikr in the ruku' position is the dhikr of the sajda position in salãh as Subhana Rabbiya al-A'la سبحان ربي الاعلى.

One should remember that a person on the true path of Islãm as a Muslim has the assigned privilege of the use of the term Rabbi as mentioned in the ruku' and sujud positions. This can be translated as 'my Sustainer'. The pronoun 'my' shows a level of acceptance. Therefore, it is similar to a person who is already accepted in the house. He or she is not an outsider but is now an insider as the word Rabbi alludes. Now, the person moves forward learning about increasing his or her rank in this house.

The constant repetition of 'Allahu Akbar' has a very close relationship with Subhana Rabbiya al-Azìm and Subhana Rabbiya al-A'la.

Allahu Akbar is the door for entering into the rooms of Subhana Rabbiya al-A'la and Subhana Rabbiya al-Azìm in this house. Allahu Akbar is the door for also entering into this house.

In this sense, Allahu Akbar is the outside door to enter the house of the Beloved ﷻ with the initial takbir of takbir tahrimi. Now, the person should follow the etiquette of being a guest in the House of the Beloved ﷻ. He or she can't talk, eat, look around, or even think of anything except the Beloved ﷻ.

Each door in this House is Allahu Akbar except the exit door. The person opens the door of Allahu Akbar and enters the living room of Subhana Rabbiya al-Azìm in ruk'u. The person waits, and sits in this room with Subhana Rabbiya al-Azìm. Then, he or she leaves this room through the door of Allahu Akbar.

Then, the person enters through another door of Allahu Akbar to the most private and secret room (haram) of Subhana Rabbiya al-A'la in sujud. Rasulullah ﷺ mentions the closest person to Allah ﷻ is in the position of sujud [5] (482). In this position more than before, we cry, miss, and beg our Beloved ﷻ.

Afterwards, we leave this private room through the door of Allahu Akbar. Yet, our remembrance and time with the Beloved ﷻ is so dense and intense that we desire to go back to spend more time with Rabbul Alamìn. We go back and open the door of Allahu Akbar and enter the private room of (haram) of Subhana Rabbiya al-A'la in sujud one more time.

In this position, we know that we may not come back again. So, we try to extend our time in sujud to spend more and more time with the Beloved ﷻ. Yet, our worldly engagements remind us that we have responsibilities. Then, we leave this private room through the door of Allahu Akbar one more time.

Depending on the time of the day, we repeat the above cycle referred to as raka' twice, three times, or four times. Each raka' is like a tawãf around the Kabah, Baytullah. Yet, in Hajj or umrah (pilgrimage), we do tawaf up to seven times- four times slowly and three times in a faster mode. Also in salãh, we do the tawãf of the House of the Beloved, Baytullah at least twice, three times, and four times with each raka' depending on the prayer time. Fajr is two raka'; magrib is three raka'; and zuhr, asr and isha are four raka'. Hajj is limited with the space and time. It should be in Mecca and at the month of Hajj. Yet, Pilgrimage of

Salah has a wider time with five-times prayer and has no limitation with optional nawafil. Pilgrimage of salãh has almost no limit with space. The person can enter the House of the Beloved at any place.

After we leave the secret room (haram) of Subhana Rabbiya al-A'la in sujud, the last place we visit in the House of the Beloved is the kitchen. One can imagine a house with an exit door located in the kitchen. In the kitchen, we eat and receive gifts before we leave the House with tahiyyat, salawat, and dua as Rasulullah ﷺ received the gifts while leaving mirãj, from the Beloved Presence of Rabbul Alamin.

Each salah is a mirãj of the person. In each salah, the person is fortunate enough to spend time with Rabbul Alamin, the Beloved ﷻ. In each salah, the person receives food and gifts before they leave.

The exit door of the House of the Beloved is Assalumu Alaykum Wa Rahmatullah.

Similar to the ending of tawaf in Hajj or umrah, the person leaves Baytullah, Kabah in maqami Ibrahim and receives gifts by making dua and prays two rakaks, gives Salam.

The person who leaves the Kabah misses the Kabah, Baytullah and wants to go back. The person who lives the salah, the House of the Beloved misses the salah and looks forward to the next one. Rasulullah ﷺ mentions that the person who awaits the next salah after finishing one and his heart is attached to the masjid will be under the shade of the Arsh of Allah ﷻ when everyone else would be in the state of fear on the Day of Judgment [2] (629) & [5] (1031).

Allah ﷻ minimally invites us five times a day to the Sacred House of Presence (Khudur). There are a lot of us who don't know the etiquette of being in Khudur. We steal in this House although the House Owner, Allah ﷻ, sees everything. Rasulullah ﷺ mentions that one of the worst types of stealing is the case of the one who is wandering mentally and physically in their prayer, salah [15].

May Allah ﷻ protect us from stealing of all kinds, Amìn.

May Allah ﷻ give us the proper adab of being in Khudur of Allah ﷻ, Amìn.

Human Value Systems as Social Constructs

The Qurãn is perfect, flawless, and complete. The discussions of skepticism and doubt are all human related concepts or social constructs.

The expression إِنَّ اللهَ لاَ يَسْتَحْيِي أَن يَضْرِبَ مَثَلاً can indicate this humanly framework of judging and valuing things. In this regard, discussion related with insects, worms, or flies can be lowly in the human realm of valuation system.

Yet, to point out this flaw in the human social construction of the world, systems, and values, Allah ﷻ really gives this example right in the beginning of the Qurãn to challenge this error in human thought process. In this case, humans have an implied assumption that if someone talks about topics considered lowly by humans, then this undertaking may not fit the nobility of the person.

In this regard, this could have been the case especially in the pre-modern societies and eras. Today, with the advancement of science, we are all amazed with the structure, order, and system in both micro and macro worlds. For an intelligent person, these examples go beyond discussions of social class implying caste systems of external nobility which lack the needed disposition of focusing internally on the essence or the content rather than assigning values according to the externalities. All of the caste systems and nobility-related renderings can somehow have relation with the internal spiritual disease of arrogance.

One should remember that we give relative values to the beings around us. One refers to this as social construction. In other words, one can claim that we use a language that we construct ourselves. This relative language is our own construction system of values through our experiences.

Allah ﷻ created everything. Everything is a creation of Allah ﷻ. The sun is a creation of Allah ﷻ. A fly is a creation of Allah ﷻ. An atom, an electron, a proton, a neutron, and a quark are all creations of Allah ﷻ. They are all under the command and order of Allah ﷻ. They are all a'bd of Allah ﷻ.

The notion of good, evil, ugly, or beautiful are all means, definitions, and values that we view in our world among the creation as another creation. All the creation is an a'bd of Allah .ﷻ This is mentioned as[116] إِن كُلُّ مَن فِي السَّمَاوَاتِ وَالْأَرْضِ إِلَّا آتِي الرَّحْمَٰنِ عَبْدًا {مريم/93}. All the creation has the absolute reality of being an a'bd of Allah ﷻ.

116. There is no one in the heavens and earth but that he comes to the Most Merciful as a servant.

All the creation has the same expected purpose of remembering this u'budiyyah while fulfilling their assigned responsibility on the earth. All of the creation recognizes and fulfills their assigned u'budiyyah except some humans and Jinn. Allah ﷻ has given the potential to humans and Jinn to exceed all of the creation in their u'budiyyah with their effort and Fadl of Allah ﷻ.

Conversely, they can be at the lowest of the low of all creation in their 'ubudiyyah with their choices. The epitome of all creation who surpassed all of the creation in 'ubudiyyah is Rasulullah ﷺ. The lowest of the low of all creation that is at the bottom in the 'ubudiyyah is Shaytān.

Golden Rules to Remember

One should remember that humans form their value systems according to their own understandings. Yet, the statement إِنَّ اللهَ لَا يَسْتَحْيِي أَن يَضْرِبَ مَثَلًا مَّا بَعُوضَةً ends all of these assumptions and wrong constructions about Allah ﷻ.

In their reality and essence, everything has a high and valuable purpose and meaning. Although some of the things in their externality may look ugly or evil, yet in their essence they have beauty and purpose in their utmost relationship purpose of being existent among the creation.

In this regard, Allah ﷻ is the Rabbul Alamin for all creation regardless of their reference point to the humans.

Sometimes, due to the balagah and the style of the speech and writing, the examples from different valuations can amplify the effects of the message.

Sometimes, describing unpleasantness, a secret, or evil has a purpose of explaining the problem, disease, and case fully. Yet, one can realize the adab of these explanations in the Qurān in that it allows the reader to receive the message without the side effects of doubts or unpleasant imaginings. In other words, the adab requires one to describe the evil or unpleasantry with modesty and balance.

It is important to use the popular speech, dialogue, terminology, and language when making da'wah and tabligh to others. Disconnect in the language can cause misunderstandings, alienation, and isolation from the message.

Hitting the Core of the Cancerous Disease and the Gamma Knife Treatment

Existence & Non-Existence

The creation of everything has alike and equal position for Allah ﷻ unlike humans' engagement of value systems which range from difficult to easy. A creation can be more complex and bigger in structure than the other as mentioned[117] لَخَلْقُ السَّمَاوَاتِ وَالْأَرْضِ أَكْبَرُ مِنْ خَلْقِ النَّاسِ وَلَكِنَّ أَكْثَرَ النَّاسِ لَا يَعْلَمُونَ {غافر/57}.

Yet, their level of creation in terms of equality is the same for Allah ﷻ. We use the term equality to avoid terms such as easy or difficult, bigger or smaller, or etc. These are all valid terms in the human realm of the constructed systems of values. The absolute actuality of this for the Transcendent Reality, Allah ﷻ is mentioned as[118] إِنَّمَا أَمْرُهُ إِذَا أَرَادَ شَيْئًا أَنْ يَقُولَ لَهُ كُنْ فَيَكُونُ {يس/82}.

One can consider here the example of a scale. If we consider two heavy objects of the same weight and place one object on one side of the scale and place the other object on the other side of the scale, then they will be equal, in balance and equilibrium. Similarly, if we consider two very light objects of the same weight, and put one of them on one side of the scale and put the other object on the other side of the scale, then they will also be equal, in balance and equilibrium as well. If we imagine the same massive star on each side of the scale, then there will still be equality regardless of their size or massiveness balancing each other. If we imagine the same lightweight fly on each side of the scale, then there will still be equality regardless of their minute size balancing each other.

Yet, if there is a tiny difference on one side of the scale, then that part of the scale will win over the other side.

Similarly, in our human renderings and approximations, one can possibly understand the notion of existence and non-existence to be similar to this equal plane on the scales of possibility, mumkinãt. Whenever and if Allah ﷻ wills as mentioned إِذَا أَرَادَ شَيْئًا, the order of كُنْ from Allah ﷻ, brings that thing into existence as mentioned فَيَكُونُ. In this

117. The creation of the heavens and earth is greater than the creation of mankind, but most of the people do not know.
118. His command is only when He intends a thing that He says to it, "Be," and it is.

regard, this thing can be a massive star or a light fly, it does not matter. Allahu A'lam.

Astagfirullah min al-su-i al-adab ma' Allah ﷻ. Oh Allah! Protect me from bad adab with You, Amìn.

The Purpose of the Qurãn Related to Present Christianity, Judaism, Buddhism and Hinduism

If one reviews the major world religions such as present Christianity, Judaism, Buddhism, and Hinduism, one can realize that the Qurãn with the teachings and practices of Rasulullah ﷺ aims to restore the original and authentic teachings about Divinity through the pillars of true monotheism, tawhid, for the original and authentic path of Allah ﷻ.

One of the diversions of Christian, Jewish, and altered scriptural theologies from the true, authentic, and original teachings of their scriptures and prophets is due to applying a human valuation system to the Transcendent Reality of Allah ﷻ.

One of the main reasons and purposes that the Qurãn was sent with Rasulullah ﷺ was to restore the a'qãi'd, creed-related teachings of these altered scriptures and prophetic teachings into their original forms as sent and revealed by Allah ﷻ.

There are many examples of this problem of human constructed value systems being applied to the Realm of the Transcendent Reality, Allah ﷻ.

One can realize that the Qurãn constantly addresses this problem of the human construction of value systems with the Realm of the Transcendent Reality, Allah ﷻ. All of the time and especially in these cases, one should really maintain one's humbleness, humility, and adab with Allah ﷻ as humans are all in need, weak, and all dependent upon Allah ﷻ.

Ayatal Kursi and Sûrah Ikhlãs as the Localized & Boost Treatment

If we take examples of two constantly repeated verses or sûrahs in the Qurãn such as Ayatal Kursi and Sûrah Ikhlas, then one can realize how these problems are addressed and treated. Below is Ayatal Kursi:[119]

119. Allah ﷻ—there is no deity except Him, the Ever-Living, the Sustainer of [all] existence. Neither drowsiness overtakes Him nor sleep. To Him belongs whatever is in the heavens and whatever is on the earth. Who is it that can intercede with Him except by His permission? He knows what is [presently] before them and what will be after them, and they encompass not a thing of His knowledge except for what He wills. His Kursi extends over the heavens and the earth, and their preservation tires Him not. And He is the Most High, the Most Great.

اللّهُ لاَ إِلَهَ إِلاَّ هُوَ الْحَيُّ الْقَيُّومُ لاَ تَأْخُذُهُ سِنَةٌ وَلاَ نَوْمٌ لَّهُ مَا فِي السَّمَاوَاتِ وَمَا فِي الأَرْضِ مَن ذَا الَّذِي يَشْفَعُ عِنْدَهُ إِلاَّ بِإِذْنِهِ يَعْلَمُ مَا بَيْنَ أَيْدِيهِمْ وَمَا خَلْفَهُمْ وَلاَ يُحِيطُونَ بِشَيْءٍ مِّنْ عِلْمِهِ إِلاَّ بِمَا شَاء وَسِعَ كُرْسِيُّهُ السَّمَاوَاتِ وَالأَرْضَ وَلاَ يَؤُودُهُ حِفْظُهُمَا وَهُوَ الْعَلِيُّ الْعَظِيمُ {البقرة/255}

Both Ayatal Kursi and Sûrah Ikhlãs hit the root disease of this cancerous tumor to treat even a metastasis of the entire body of the creed system. The approaches of the Quranic treatment of cancer and the modern medical treatment of cancer are different. The Quranic treatment replaces the cancerous cells-in a way similar to the very precise gamma knife treatment- with healthy and benign cells appropriate to that tissue. The medical modern treatment only kills these cells without much replacement. Yet, the body that Allah ﷻ has created is expected to replace these death cells with the benign cells.

In the physical body of cancer, the doer is Allah ﷻ by regenerating the benign cells. In the spiritual cancerous disease of the heart and mind, the doer is Allah ﷻ with the treatment of the Qurãn and Rasulullah ﷺ. All of the teachings of Rasulullah ﷺ are revelation from Allah ﷻ. Hadith and sunnah of Rasulullah saw are called gayru-matluw, unrecited revelation unlike the required disposition of the Qurãn as the recited revelation. One can see below some of the details of these details with their treatment Ayatal Kursi.

Disease Type	Treatment
Multiplicity, trinity, duality	اللّهُ لاَ إِلَهَ إِلاَّ هُوَ True Monotheism, One and Unique Creator, Allah ﷻ.
Absent/passive God	الْحَيُّ الْقَيُّومُ Constantly Intervening, Full Active, Full Alive, Infinite Allah ﷻ.
Human qualities for God such as sleeping, unawareness	لاَ تَأْخُذُهُ سِنَةٌ وَلاَ نَوْمٌ Always in Full Control, Always in Full Awareness, Allah ﷻ.
Randomness, chaos, without ownership	لَّهُ مَا فِي السَّمَاوَاتِ وَمَا فِي الأَرْضِ Full Ownership, Control, Structure, Order as set by Allah ﷻ.
Proximity and piety related partnership with God	مَن ذَا الَّذِي يَشْفَعُ عِنْدَهُ إِلاَّ بِإِذْنِهِ No Partnership in Authority and Decision Making. Only and except by the ones that Allah ﷻ gives permission or enablement.

Absence of Knowledge of God with time boundaries and other boundaries	يَعْلَمُ مَا بَيْنَ أَيْدِيهِمْ وَمَا خَلْفَهُمْ Full Control of Knowledge without any time boundaries and without any blockage of concepts such as internal or external, or obvious or secret.
Absolute and True Knowledge can be acquired only by mind. Therefore, mind or intellect is above the wahiy/revelation.	وَلاَ يُحِيطُونَ بِشَيْءٍ مِّنْ عِلْمِهِ إِلاَّ بِمَا شَاء True and Absolute Knowledge given only by Allah ﷻ. An ummi can have more true and absolute knowledge given by Allah ﷻ as compared to an educated philosopher as a miracle similar to the case of Rasulullah ﷺ. True knowledge necessitates mind and humbleness/humility with the enablement, Fadl of Allah ﷻ.
This universe, earth, and galaxies are only the ones. We discovered everything. Therefore, we are powerful.	وَسِعَ كُرْسِيُّهُ السَّمَاوَاتِ وَالأَرْضَ This universe, earth, space, and galaxies that you know with your limited knowledge are nothing compared to the Dominion, Kursi of Allah ﷻ, so be Humble!
God became tired and rested.	وَلاَ يَؤُودُهُ حِفْظُهُمَا Allah ﷻ is far beyond human concepts of social constructs such as being tired due to difficulty. Human valuation and constructs are NOT valid in the Realm of Transcendent Reality.
Applying human value systems to the Realm of Transcendent Reality	وَلاَ يَؤُودُهُ حِفْظُهُمَا وَهُوَ الْعَلِيُّ الْعَظِيمُ {البقرة/255} Allah ﷻ is far beyond and always higher than human constructions of any type of human valuation systems, so be humble and submit yourself to Allah ﷻ on the path of the Qurān with the sunnah of Rasulullah ﷺ.

A similar above analysis can be made for Sûrah Ikhlas to hit the root disease of a cancer carried by many[120]. قُلْ هُوَ اللَّهُ أَحَدٌ {الإخلاص/1} اللَّهُ الصَّمَدُ {الإخلاص/2} لَمْ يَلِدْ وَلَمْ يُولَدْ {الإخلاص/3} وَلَمْ يَكُن لَّهُ كُفُوًا أَحَدٌ {الإخلاص/4}

120. 1. Say, "He is Allah ﷻ, [who is] One, 2. Allah ﷻ, the Eternal Refuge. 3. He neither begets nor is born, 4. Nor is there to Him any equivalent."

Disease Type	Treatment
Illusional monotheism: such as trinity, multiplicity as reflected in deities as represented with different attributes of the same reality, or not explicitly naming Allah ﷻ, the One but using metaphors such as nature, the one, etc.	قُلْ هُوَ اللَّهُ أَحَدٌ {الإخلاص/1} Allah ﷻ is One and Unique—Have the true tawhid. Don't mix illusions with realities.
Causes as the real doers. Therefore, being dependent on the causes, multiplicities, rather than being only dependent on Allah ﷻ.	اللَّهُ الصَّمَدُ {الإخلاص/2} Allah ﷻ is the only Independent Being. Everything is dependent on Allah ﷻ.
Applying human value system to God such as birth, parenthood, spouse, etc.	لَمْ يَلِدْ وَلَمْ يُولَدْ {الإخلاص/3} Allah ﷻ is Unique and far beyond the values and necessities of creation.
Applying human value systems to the Realm of Transcendent Reality	وَلَمْ يَكُن لَّهُ كُفُوًا أَحَدٌ {الإخلاص/4} Carve into your little mind and heart that Allah ﷻ is One and Unique. There is no other being similar to Allah ﷻ.

One can find other, similar, or different diseases addressed in the Qurãn with more treatment sessions. As we sometimes cannot read the entire Qurãn to address all of these diseases, Rasulullah ﷺ suggests reading Sûrah Ikhlas three times for this is equivalent to reading all of the Qurãn in order to address all of the diseases [5] (hadith # 811). Rasulullah ﷺ also suggests reading Ayatal Kursi at least five times a day after each prayer to take preventive measures as a protection from all of the diseases of the heart, mind, and body [15] (hadith # 7406).

Human Language, Reductionism, & the Role of the Scholars

One should remember that the Qurãn uses the human world's realities of language to address the problems and offer their solutions. If the Qurãn discussed in a very non-understandable and theoretical language, there would have been a disconnect from the perspectives of humans in terms of comprehension and accessibility. Therefore, as people specialize in each field including the science of religion, the technical words referred to as 'istilah' have a perfect meaning for the experts who are few. This is mentioned as[121] {العنكبوت/43} وَتِلْكَ الْأَمْثَالُ نَضْرِبُهَا لِلنَّاسِ وَمَا يَعْقِلُهَا إِلَّا الْعَالِمُونَ

121. And these examples We present to the people, but none will understand them except those of knowledge.

Yet, the majority may not understand what the reality and essence is. In this position, the experts have the responsibility of explaining these in the reductive language of the ʿamm for the general population so that the people are not misguided. This duty is very critical and should even be maintained at the times of dire need as mentioned[122] وَمَا كَانَ الْمُؤْمِنُونَ لِيَنفِرُواْ كَآفَّةً فَلَوْلاَ نَفَرَ مِن كُلِّ فِرْقَةٍ مِّنْهُمْ طَآئِفَةٌ لِّيَتَفَقَّهُواْ فِي الدِّينِ وَلِيُنذِرُواْ قَوْمَهُمْ إِذَا رَجَعُواْ إِلَيْهِمْ لَعَلَّهُمْ يَحْذَرُونَ {التوبة/122}.

In reality, the positions of the prophets serve this purpose. In reality, the prophets know and have the highest level of imān and marifatullah. Rasulullah ﷺ mentions, "If you knew what I knew, you would laugh less and cry more." [4] In this regard, the position of the prophets, ulama, and teachers have the responsibility of always reducing and adapting what they understand of the breezes of the Divine knowledge and experience to the comprehension level of the humans.

One should remember that in the causality of humans, humans are attracted to the content if they have any relevance, understanding, and connection with it. Therefore, adapting the language for humans in the contents of the Qurān, in hadith, and in the practices of Rasulullah ﷺ is present with a purposeful hikmah, wisdom. Most people do not understand the scientific language of technicalities. They understand teachings in their popular language of culture and time.

In other words, everyone and everything speaks in their own language of habitat. Humans talk and understand within the social construct system of language in their habitat. The Qurān primarily addresses humans and therefore the Qurān uses a language that they would understand.

Birds view the world according to their understanding. They understand Divinity, Tawhid in Allah ﷻ in their own language. This is mentioned in[123] أَلَّا يَسْجُدُوا لِلَّهِ الَّذِي يُخْرِجُ الْخَبْءَ فِي السَّمَاوَاتِ وَالْأَرْضِ وَيَعْلَمُ مَا تُخْفُونَ وَمَا تُعْلِنُونَ {النمل/25} اللَّهُ لَا إِلَٰهَ إِلَّا هُوَ رَبُّ الْعَرْشِ الْعَظِيمِ {النمل/26}. The word الْخَبْءَ is a critical food item for the birds. By using its valuation system of importance for their sustenance (rizq), the hoopoe bird gives an example from an item that is so critical for the species of birds. Then, the

---

122. And it is not for the believers to go forth [to battle] all at once. For there should separate from every division of them a group [remaining] to obtain understanding in the religion and warn their people when they return to them that they might be cautious.

123. 25. [And] so they do not prostrate to Allah ﷻ, who brings forth what is hidden within the heavens and the earth and knows what you conceal and what you declare—26. Allah ﷻ—there is no deity except Him, Lord of the Great Throne."

bird very well and precisely explains the true Tawhid in Allah . This is mentioned as .{النمل/26} اللَّهُ لَا إِلَٰهَ إِلَّا هُوَ رَبُّ الْعَرْشِ الْعَظِيمِ SubhanAllah!

The Cookies and the Qurãn

The maqãsid of the Qurãn is the guidance of the 'ãmm, the general audience. The general audience has an average education level of understanding and they are not intellectuals or scholars. The general audience may not be able to see obvious realities. When they are not familiar with a concept, then they don't understand it.

In other words, the effort of learning can come with higher education levels. The concepts in the popular language such as 'bread and butter occupations' indicate the monotonous routines of work that shape the people's attitudes and traits. In this regard, many people have a resistance to change in order to not break their affinity to these routines that form a comfort zone for the person.

In this regard, Allah as a Rahmah and Fadl gives examples in the Qurãn with the items that are familiar to the general public audience. A fly, a spider, a bee, a cow, rain, and harvest are all themes displayed in the Qurãn to address the general public with the language that they know. In this known language, a concept can be introduced to the readers in order for them to reflect and ponder about their routines.

Today, this style can have different names in different disciplines. For example, in business or marketing, one can call this 'getting the customer in the door' by using some attractive techniques for the client. In the writing industry, one can refer to this as 'the opener', utilizing the cover or the title of the book to cause the reader to give attention to this book. Especially, one can consider today's online industries such as Amazon. By using the applications referred to as 'cookies', the online companies push the items depending on the preferences of the customers.

Allah knows us fully, as Allah is our Creator and Maker. As mentioned[124] وَعِندَهُ مَفَاتِحُ الْغَيْبِ لَا يَعْلَمُهَا إِلَّا هُوَ وَيَعْلَمُ مَا فِي الْبَرِّ وَالْبَحْرِ وَمَا تَسْقُطُ

124. And with Him are the keys of the unseen; none knows them except Him. And He knows what is on the land and in the sea. Not a leaf falls but that He knows it. And no grain is there within the darknesses of the earth and no moist or dry [thing] but that it is [written] in a clear record.

مِن وَرَقَةٍ إِلاَّ يَعْلَمُهَا وَلاَ حَبَّةٍ فِي ظُلُمَاتِ الأَرْضِ وَلاَ رَطْبٍ وَلاَ يَابِسٍ إِلاَّ فِي كِتَابٍ مُّبِينٍ {الأنعام/59}

The Qurān includes fully, and perfectly all the words, emotions, excitations, and concepts attracting each individual's attention among all of the billions of people today and in the past.

The personal openings of the Qurān for a person with any ayah, with a sûrah, with a word or even with a letter can be similar to the applications referred to as 'cookies' that the online companies display according to the person's possible interests and needs depending on one's online search history. In this sense, Allah ﷻ knows fully our cookies in our minds and hearts all of the time.Therefore, the Qurān is designed and bestowed on us by Allah ﷻ in such a way that one can more fully satisfy one's needs with the Qurān as compared to anything else. There are a lot of ayahs in the Qurān that can allude to this reality.

Misleading Respect and True Adab with Allah ﷻ

The approach of distancing the understanding of God from lowly things as defined by humans can have different perspectives.

If the people want to respect and have adab with Allah ﷻ and remove all of the wrong and incorrect renderings and constructions about Allah ﷻ, then this is called tanzìh. The dhikr of SubhanAllah can indicate these meanings. This stance is required and is part of one's imān.

If some groups and people approach to deny the creation of evil-seeming incidents, and ugly and lowly beings from Allah ﷻ, then this can have some problematic perspectives.

Everything is created by Allah ﷻ. Allah ﷻ is in control and is the authority of creating everything including the incidents and beings.

There can be some ugly and undesired beings in the human constructions such as snakes, mice, some types of dogs, flies, or other beings that are considered lowly and undesired by humans. Yet, they are all created by Allah ﷻ. They have a purpose and they recognize Allah ﷻ.

There is a reason why humans consider them evil and dislike them. Yet, Allah ﷻ creates everything with a purpose.

Similarly, the evil-seeming incidents are allowed and created by Allah ﷻ. Yet, their existence and arrival into our reality is and can be due to the people's engagement of causality. Allah ﷻ allows the causality as part of the free will execution allowed to humans in this world.

The expression إِنَّ اللَّهَ لاَ يَسْتَحْيِي أَن يَضْرِبَ مَثَلاً مَّا بَعُوضَةً فَمَا فَوْقَهَا hits the core of this problem.

Some people with a good-seeming intention can only relate good-looking beings and incidents to Allah ﷻ. This can be well understood and fully agreed upon with the notions of adab.

The practice of a Muslim not making dhikr in the bathroom can be an example of this. The notion of a Muslim woman not touching the Qurãn in the cycles of physical impurity can be another example of this.

Yet, Allah ﷻ is aware of what the person does in the bathroom and Allah ﷻ creates, controls, and maintains the means of excretion system in a human body through small and large intestines, bladder, and other amazing excretion systems as maintained by Rabbul Alamin. Similarly, a woman goes through a very complicated physical cleansing process in her uterus as maintained by Rabbul Alamin.

Now, if Allah ﷻ is al-Bãtin, al-Zãhir, al-Alìm, al-Khabìr, al-Hafiz, and our Rabb, why do we have the above formalities of not making dhikr or touching the Qurãn at all times?

The answer is **adab with Allah ﷻ.**

Adab with Allah ﷻ requires having modesty with Allah ﷻ. Modesty is part of the imãn.

Adab requires loving Allah ﷻ. Loving Allah ﷻ is part of the imãn.

Adab requires being fearful of Allah ﷻ, of not displeasing Allah ﷻ. Having the fear of displeasing Allah ﷻ is the state of ihsãn.

There are some awliya of Allah SWT who may not engage themselves with even permissible, halal items due to a fear of displeasing Allah ﷻ although they may find allowances from different rulings that would allow themselves to implement a permissibility. Yet, the fear of displeasing Allah ﷻ can put them in the state of being shy from Allah ﷻ.

As Allah ﷻ did so much for the person, the person can always be in the state of constantly asking oneself: "Am I displeasing Allah ﷻ as Allah ﷻ is watching me? Did Allah ﷻ turn away from me?" meaning "Is Allah ﷻ displeased with me?"

There is the constant worry and concern of the person. "Am I displeasing Allah ﷻ currently with what I am doing, with what I am thinking, with what I am saying?"

This is the station, the maqãm of ihsãn, maqãm of modesty and having haya with Allah ﷻ.

This maqam is having adab with Allah ﷻ.

Allahumma Ja'alna minhum, Amìn. اللهم جعلنا منهم، آمين

Maqams, stations are permanent. Hãl, states are temporary. On the spiritual path, one aims to turn one's state into station, one's hãl into maqãm with the Fadl and Tawfik of Allah ﷻ. Maqãm of ihsãn is the highest level that one can achieve.

There are people from the awliya who were very shy going into the bathroom and relieving themselves and exposing their awrah. This is the maqam of their adab with Allah ﷻ.

Rasulullah ﷺ did not take his clothes off when he ﷺ used to take a shower. It was narrated that no one looked at the private parts of Rasulullah ﷺ. This is natural embodiment of haya, modesty, with Allah ﷻ as he ﷺ peaked in every aspect of imãn.

Allahumma Ja'alna man attibu sabila Habibuk ﷺ, Amìn. اللهم جعلنا مَن اتبع سَبِيل حبِيبِّك صلى الله عليه وسلم

In this regard, outward and external actions of respect or adab can elevate the person in his or her relationship with Allah ﷻ.

Yet, we follow the Qurãn, the sunnah of Rasulullah ﷺ and the ways of our pious salaf in understanding the shi'ar of Allah ﷻ to understand what adab and respect require and how to implement them.

Going back to our original discussion, assuming the absence of Allah ﷻ in relation to ugly-looking or evil-rendering beings or incidents can cause deep theological problems in the pillars of imãn. This happened in the renderings of other religions such as Christianity, Judaism, and in prior teachings of the prophets.

The notions of Greek mythological deities, pre-Islamic Meccan societies of deities through idol worshipping, the dualities of Satanism giving power to Shaytãn are further extreme examples of this notion of not understanding appropriation of adab in regard to one's true relationship with Allah ﷻ through the discourses of tawhid.

These groups slowly alienated themselves from tawhid with good-looking intentions. Yet, they diverged from the core and original teachings of imãn and tawhid as instructed by their prophets and scriptures from Allah ﷻ.

True Nobility

When we review the life of Rasulullah ﷺ, one can realize true understanding of nobility and adab. Nobility in this case is not the classical definition of 'belonging to a hereditary class with a high social or political stance [2]. Nobility is not the case of representation of aristocracy being in the highest class due to hereditary titles or offices' [2].

Nobility of Rasulullah ﷺ has two perspectives. One is his own ﷺ build up of character traits before and after Islãm. The other is his ﷺ absolute and permanent nobility given by Allah ﷻ due to being the Prophet of Allah ﷻ.

Both are related and complementary.

Rasulullah ﷺ had fame and a reputation for being the one who was trustworthy before and after Islãm. This was a sign of true nobility.

Rasulullah ﷺ had fame and a reputation for having calmness, patience, tranquility, kindness, care, and serenity before and after Islãm. These were all signs of true nobility.

Rasulullah ﷺ had fame and a reputation for altruism, preferring others over himself in all manners of wealth and worldly engagements before and after Islãm. This was a sign of true nobility.

Unlike the classical definitions of nobility, Rasulullah ﷺ was eating with the poor and weak. This was the true sign of nobility.

Rasulullah ﷺ preferred hunger and fed others. This was the true sign of nobility.

Rasulullah ﷺ valued and appreciated everything in life from Allah ﷻ. He ﷺ appreciated even simple-looking tools such as a mirror and hair brush and named them similar to a person's name to show appreciation and not belittle anything. This was the true sign of nobility.

Rasulullah ﷺ listened to the problems of everyone including humans, animals, and trees.

Rasulullah ﷺ engaged in talking with animals. Some of these animals were complaining about their owner's abuse. Some of these animals were mules or donkeys which were defined as lowly creatures in the society. Yet, Rasulullah ﷺ took their problems seriously and addressed these issues with their owners. This was the true sign of nobility.

Rasulullah ﷺ engaged himself with zeal, desire, and aspiration with the part of the society that was deemed or considered to be low-class. This was the true sign of nobility.

A black sahabah who was not good-looking seemed to be experiencing some alienation in the social life due to his appearance and poverty. One day, Rasulullah ﷺ hugged him and said, "I have someone with me who has a very high value with Allah ﷻ" in order to comfort this broken-hearted sahabah. He ﷺ constantly showed others the true value of people and things. This was the true sign of nobility.

An old woman used to clean the masjid. She passed away. The sahabah did not want to inform Rasulullah ﷺ with the intention of not disturbing him because Rasulullah ﷺ was busy as he ﷺ was similar to the president of the newly built country. When he ﷺ found out about her demise, he did not seem to be happy that the sahabah did not inform him ﷺ. He ﷺ went to her grave and prayed her janazah prayer again and talked to her in her grave. This was the true sign of nobility.

The reality of the absolute, permanent, and unchanging title of the Prophet ﷺ as the Noble ﷺ has become emergent to our realm when Allah ﷻ assigned and revealed his prophethood ﷺ.

Allah ﷻ, Rabbul Alamìn gave him different titles, praised, and eased Rasulullah ﷺ due to his overarching nobility as mentioned in the Qurãn. One can amazingly review and ponder upon the below ayahs to realize this Noble position of Rasulullah ﷺ given by Allah ﷻ:

لَقَدْ جَاءكُمْ رَسُولٌ مِّنْ أَنفُسِكُمْ عَزِيزٌ عَلَيْهِ مَا عَنِتُّمْ حَرِيصٌ عَلَيْكُم بِالْمُؤْمِنِينَ رَؤُوفٌ رَّحِيمٌ {التوبة/128}[125]

فَلَعَلَّكَ بَاخِعٌ نَّفْسَكَ عَلَى آثَارِهِمْ إِن لَّمْ يُؤْمِنُوا بِهَذَا الْحَدِيثِ أَسَفًا {الكهف/6}[126]

لَعَلَّكَ بَاخِعٌ نَّفْسَكَ أَلَّا يَكُونُوا مُؤْمِنِينَ {الشعراء/3}[127]

Allahumma Salli Ala Sayyidina wa Habibina Muhammad Kama Salayta ala sayyidina Ibrahim wa ala ali sayyidina Ibrahim innaka Hamidun Majid. اللهم صلى على سيدنا و حبيبنا محمد كما صليت على سيدنا ابراهيم وعلى آل سيدنا ابراهيم انك حميد مجيد

Allahumma Inna Asaluka ma salaka muhammadun ﷺ wa na'uzu bika masata'zu Muhammadan ﷺ. اللهم إنّا أسالك مَا سَالك مُحمد صلى الله عليه وسلم وأعُوذبِكَ مَستَعاذ مُحمد صلى الله عليه وسلم...

125. There has certainly come to you a Messenger from among yourselves. Grievous to him is what you suffer; [he is] concerned over you and to the believers is kind and merciful.

126. Then perhaps you would kill yourself through grief over them, [O Muhammad ﷺ], if they do not believe in this message, [and] out of sorrow.

127. Perhaps, [O Muhammad ﷺ], you would kill yourself with grief that they will not be believers.

Allahumma Rabbi Hazihi Da'watul Ta'amah Wa Salatil Qaimah, Ati Sayyidina Muhammadan al-Wasilata wal Fadila, wa ba'aus maqaman mahmudan allazi wa'adah innaka la tukhlifil mi'ad اللهم رب هذه الدعوة التامة والصلاة القائمة، آتى سيدنا محمد الوسيلة والفضيلة،و بعث مقام محموداً الذى وعدته انك لا تخلف الميعاد

Race, Gender, & Ethnicity

When we analyze the expression وَيَقْطَعُونَ مَا أَمَرَ اللهُ بِهِ أَن يُوصَلَ, the tafãsir especially mentions the importance of keeping the bonds among family members as sila-rahim and other fellows. The absence of non-bonding can cause chaos, fitnah as mentioned وَيُفْسِدُونَ فِي الأَرْضِ.

In this regard, if we analyze the expression الَّذِينَ يَنقُضُونَ عَهْدَ اللهِ مِن بَعْدِ مِيثَاقِهِ وَيَقْطَعُونَ مَا أَمَرَ اللهُ بِهِ أَن يُوصَلَ in the ayah, this teaching really hits both the problem and the solution in our modern-day problems related to race, ethnicity, and gender.

When we look at today's societies, we find many people who are not happy about who they are and what they have. This is another level of kufr, lack of appreciation that has direct relation to imãn.

Specifically, people complain about their ethnicities, races, genders, or backgrounds as all are given by Allah ﷻ. We did not have a choice at our birth about our bodily and physical appearances. Normalizing this with valuation and self-esteem is critical. Accepting and valuing our bodies with their birth-related choices are the means of showing respect to Allah ﷻ.

The purpose of religion is to instill the realization of our humanness. Our humanness requires dependency. Our humanness requires accepting that control of most of the things in our life is out of our own control.

Our full dependency is on Allah ﷻ. We are pleased with all of the choices that Allah ﷻ made for us. We are thankful for and appreciate all of the Divine Choices. We appreciate and constantly thank Rabbul Alamin. We don't complain about the Divine Choices. Complaints against the qadar and qadah can lead to kufr.

The representation of level of complaints can be at different levels including one changing or imitating one's identity. Also, we can witness one being so proud about one's given identity with inclusivity that the person sees others as lowly or considers them to be of a lower class.

This leads to racism, discrimination, and a caste system of categorizing people according to their externalities.

Then, the clashes and chaos start. Hatred is instilled in people.

Modern approaches to studies of race, ethnicity, and gender sometimes indicate these implicit problems of de-valuation and loss of self-esteem for the Divine choices made for us.

In this regard, if we explore the expression الَّذِينَ يَنقُضُونَ عَهْدَ اللَّهِ مِن بَعْدِ مِيثَاقِهِ وَيَقْطَعُونَ مَا أَمَرَ اللَّهُ بِهِ أَن يُوصَلَ in the ayah, this stance really hits both the problem and the solution.

In addition, Allah ﷻ explicitly mentions[128] يَا أَيُّهَا النَّاسُ إِنَّا خَلَقْنَاكُم مِّن ذَكَرٍ وَأُنثَى وَجَعَلْنَاكُمْ شُعُوبًا وَقَبَائِلَ لِتَعَارَفُوا إِنَّ أَكْرَمَكُمْ عِندَ اللَّهِ أَتْقَاكُمْ إِنَّ اللَّهَ عَلِيمٌ خَبِيرٌ {الحجرات/13}. The diversities have the purpose of knowing each other with different externalities. This does not mean that one is better than the other. This does not mean that one is at a higher status than the other.

The categorization of virtue or status is only known and judged by God, Allah ﷻ. This invisible, real status of the person is within one's stance of appreciation of the One, Allah ﷻ with piety and in one's carrying of this appreciation to all other fellow beings with ethics and morality. In this valuation system, no one knows the real value of each person except Allah ﷻ. The physical death of the person uncovers the reality of the person to himself or herself.

Humans have no right or knowledge to judge people. Judging or categorizing them to be at a lower level is due to arrogance. One of the main objectives of the religion is the open declaration of war against arrogance in a person. Arrogance includes the dishonest claims of a person to what he doesn't own.

If one is going to have an opinion of another person, the only allowed and encouraged way is to view the other person as a friend of God, who can be higher in virtue and piety than this person. This is in order to instill humbleness and humility in this person. This is not to sanctify the person or divinize another person, concept, or being other than God, Allah ﷻ.

In this perspective, a non-Muslim can have a higher value. The person doesn't how each person will end his or her life journey. A pious

128. O mankind, indeed We have created you from male and female and made you peoples and tribes that you may know one another. Indeed, the most noble of you in the sight of Allah ﷻ is the most righteous of you. Indeed, Allah ﷻ is Knowing and Acquainted.

person can end up being an evil person and meet Allah ﷻ with his or her death in that state. May Allah ﷻ protect us, Amìn.

On the other hand, a person of kufr and evil can become a person of imãn and virtue before he or she dies with the Fadl and Rahmah of Allah ﷻ and his or her journey in that state.

Therefore, a non-judgmental stance is always the safest disposition. At the same time, it is always critical to think good about others. One scholar mentions, [16] "Be the lawyer of others and the prosecutor of your own evil ego-self." This stance gives the person the perspective of a non-aggressive attitude toward social, family, and professional relationships. This stance can help the person to develop the inner self.

When we analyze the expression[129] وَيَقْطَعُونَ مَا أَمَرَ اللَّهُ بِهِ أَن يُوصَلَ وَيُفْسِدُونَ فِي الأَرْضِ أُولَئِكَ هُمُ الْخَاسِرُونَ {البقرة/27}, one can deduce that generally the action of وَيَقْطَعُونَ, cutting can indicate destruction, mischief, and chaos. This is the opposite of uniting, keeping, maintaining, and building which can indicate structure, order, achievement, happiness and positive openings in this life and in the afterlife.

If we analyze this concept, the modern age of physical construction can indicate positive outcomes. There is an action for potential outcomes in this world and in the afterlife. Yet, all of the positive outcomes are expected to lead to humbleness. If they lead to arrogance, then these positive-seeming constructions can be in reality illusional, and leading to the real destruction of the person with arrogance. This happened in the past when people were misled by their own arrogance as mentioned[130] فَأَمَّا عَادٌ فَاسْتَكْبَرُوا فِي الْأَرْضِ بِغَيْرِ الْحَقِّ وَقَالُوا مَنْ أَشَدُّ مِنَّا قُوَّةً أَوَلَمْ يَرَوْا أَنَّ اللَّهَ الَّذِي خَلَقَهُمْ هُوَ أَشَدُّ مِنْهُمْ قُوَّةً وَكَانُوا بِآيَاتِنَا يَجْحَدُونَ {فصلت/15}.

Age, Maturity, & Pedagogy of Endless Childhood

In human values, historically, children were viewed as the source of not having proper intelligence or of being adequate in rationality. Yet, the Quranic approach and the sunnah, the practices of Rasulullah ﷺ show that everyone can be addressed depending on the audience.

129. How can you disbelieve in Allah ﷻ when you were lifeless and He brought you to life; then He will cause you to die, then He will bring you [back] to life, and then to Him you will be returned.

130. As for 'Aad, they were arrogant upon the earth without right and said, "Who is greater than us in strength?" Did they not consider that Allah ﷻ who created them was greater than them in strength? But they were rejecting Our signs.

Changing the way of addressing and explaining the Divine teachings to children can be similar to explaining them to a philosopher. The way of delivery of the knowledge and the details of the content may change, but they are still an audience with intelligence and logic who need to be addressed.

Similarly, a fly or a galaxy both show Allah ﷻ when one analyzes them, regardless of their size and valuation among humans.

The general public can be like children in their understanding as compared to the scholars. Some of the scholars are like children compared to the elite scholars of taqwa and understanding. The knowledge of some of the elite scholars, even the prophets, can be insufficient in some cases as compared to the ones with knowledge and enablement granted by Allah .ﷻ One can remember the story of Khidr as and Musa as. Although Musa as was the elite prophet of Allah ,ﷻ there was still a limitation and boundary of his knowledge as mentioned[131] وَلَا يُحِيطُونَ وَلاَ يُحِيطُونَ بِشَيْءٍ مِّنْ عِلْمِهِ إِلاَّ بِمَا شَاء وَسِعَ كُرْسِيُّهُ السَّمَاوَاتِ وَالأَرْضَin بِشَيْءٍ مِّنْ عِلْمِهِ .وَلاَ يَؤُودُهُ حِفْظُهُمَا وَهُوَ الْعَلِيُّ الْعَظِيمُ {البقرة/255}

Musa as did not mind being a student. Being a good teacher encompasses acting with wisdom, patience, knowing the level of your student, and speaking according to the knowledge of the person as mentioned[132] قَالَ إِنَّكَ لَن تَسْتَطِيعَ مَعِيَ صَبْرًا {الكهف/67} وَكَيْفَ تَصْبِرُ عَلَى مَا لَمْ تُحِطْ بِهِ خُبْرًا {الكهف/68}

Being a student most of the time brings the act of childhood behavior.

Most of the time, students exhibit childish behavior. This behavior can entail impatience, questioning, or commenting at inappropriate times without patience.

Yet, childish behavior has two branches. One is the trait of being humble and having humility with an attitude of 'please give me one more chance' or 'I won't do it again'. This can show humbleness, humility, and learning from one's mistakes. The appropriate behavior of this category is keeping silent when one is at fault or not commenting or making

131. and they encompass not a thing of His knowledge except for what He wills. His Kursi extends over the heavens and the earth, and their preservation tires Him not. And He is the Most High, the Most Great.

132. 67.He said, "Indeed, with me you will never be able to have patience. 68. And how can you have patience for what you do not encompass in knowledge?"

negative face expressions as these attitudes are very common in some cultures.

The other is the attitude of arrogance- 'I am right. I don't care'. This shows arrogance, vanity, conceit, but not learning from the mistakes. The following negative behavior of this category is argumentation with the teacher with demagogy or making negative face expressions, or talking under the tongue or making giybah.

One can remember the interaction of the angels with Allah ﷻ questioning the creation of humans, and Adam as with Allah ﷻ asking forgiveness after making a mistake representing the first category. One can also remember the interaction of Musa as with Khidr as is in this first category as well.

One can remember the comment and questioning of Shaytãn about the creation of Adam as and his absence of adab with Rabbul alamin as can be in the second category.

We should remember that all of us exhibit childish behavior according to another level of knowledge. Allah ﷻ has the absolute knowledge as mentioned[133] يَعْلَمُ مَا بَيْنَ أَيْدِيهِمْ وَمَا خَلْفَهُمْ in يَعْلَمُ مَا بَيْنَ أَيْدِيهِمْ وَمَا خَلْفَهُمْ وَلاَ يُحِيطُونَ بِشَيْءٍ مِّنْ عِلْمِهِ إِلاَّ بِمَا شَاء وَسِعَ كُرْسِيُّهُ السَّمَاوَاتِ وَالأَرْضَ وَلاَ يَؤُودُهُ حِفْظُهُمَا وَهُوَ الْعَلِيُّ الْعَظِيمُ {البقرة/255}. We all exhibit some type of childish behavior and attitudes or inadequate knowledge about mar'ifah of Allah ﷻ.

The peak and epitome of maturity and insan kamìl in this regard is Rasulullah ﷺ, al-Habìb, al-Mustafa ﷺ. One of the proofs for this besides many is his position ﷺ with Rabbul Alamìn on the Day of Judgment. When everyone, including the prophets, are in such a state of fear, Rasulullah ﷺ has the highest level of spiritual maturity, experience, and knowledge of Allah ﷻ with humbleness and humility in front of Rabbul Alamìn. He ﷺ is the only who can communicate with Rabbul Alamìn, al-Azìz, al-Gaffãr, al-Mutã'l, al-Wahid, al-Qahhãr.

According to their levels, Allah ﷻ grants some people the absence of fear, panic, and anxiety under the Arsh of Allah ﷻ on that Day [2] (hadith #629) & [5] (hadith # 1031). For example, a person whose heart is attached to the masjid or a pious youth are some of them

133. He knows what is [presently] before them and what will be after them, and they encompass not a thing of His knowledge except for what He wills. His Kursi extends over the heavens and the earth, and their preservation tires Him not. And He is the Most High, the Most Great.

according to the hadith (hadith #629) & [5] (hadith # 1031). Allahumma Ja'alna Minhum.

Rasulullah ﷺ with humbleness, humility, and at the same with spiritual maturity, experience, and knowledge of Allah ﷻ, marifatullah goes to sajdah, begs, and cries for his ﷺ ummah, to take them from the Jahannam.

SubhanAllah! This is the Epitome and Peak Point of Spiritual Maturity, Insan-I Kamil! Rasulullah is at the highest level among all of creation as a proof of his ﷺ communication and relation with Rabbul Alamin.

Therefore, La ilaha illa Allah ﷻ which is tawhid is adjacent to Muhammadun Rasulullah ﷺ in La ilaha illa Allah Muhammadun Rasulullah.

In this sense, Rasulullah ﷺ is the Epitome and Peak Point of Embodiment of Tawhid.

Yet, with the permission of Allah ﷻ, he ﷺ is granted to remove everyone who has a speck of tawhid, that is La ilaha illa Allah, from Jahannam on the Day of Judgment.

The Epitome and Source of the teaching of Tawhid, Rasulullah ﷺ, saves like an umm, ummi or a mother all of the people who have these tiny specks of tawhid as if a mother was saving children from fire.

In one hadith, Rasulullah ﷺ mentions this point of having the highest taqwa and knowing Allah ﷻ the most, yet he engaged himself with worldly engagements [21]. In this sense, the position of Rasulullah ﷺ is like a teacher for the ummah and we are all his ﷺ students with different childish behaviors for Rasulullah ﷺ. Yet, Rasulullah ﷺ did realize this in us and engaged with humans by lowering his status as part of being a good teacher.

Selection of Animals in the Qurãn

If we one reviews the selected animals in the Qurãn, one can realize that one of the common themes is that the mentioned animals all have accessibility to the reader. In other words, all of the animals are common animals in all different parts of the world, in different climates and habitats. In this sense, the Qurãn as the universal of the Book of Allah ﷻ until the End of Days again establishes universality, accessibility, and inclusivity in all the contents and in specific knowledge such as in the selection of animals.

In this regard, this ayah mentions a fly or a mosquito. This animal is known by all humans all over the world. Similarly, ants, spiders, dogs, donkeys, horses, and cows especially as one of the sources of milk and dairy products such as cheese, sheep, bees as the source of honey, and birds. There is a general encouragement to study the anatomy, physiology, and other features of these animals within their interaction with humans and in their position in the habitat.

One can see the specific mention of some of the animals although, today, the accessibility of these animals can be limited due to the specific locations of climate and habitat for these animals. Camels can be one of the examples. Yet, their mention in the Qurãn can be especially due to the special features in their creation as mentioned for the camel such as {الغاشية/17} أَفَلَا يَنظُرُونَ إِلَى الْإِبِلِ كَيْفَ خُلِقَتْ. In this sense, there is an encouragement to study the anatomy, physiology, and other features of the camel especially within their interaction with humans and in their position in the habitat.

There is the specific mention of the crow (ghurãb) (غراب) among the birds to indicate its position in the knowledge of the Islamic burial ceremony to teach humans and to humble them. A disliked, possibly disgusting animal and frowned upon bird by humans, such as the crow, who eats the dead bodies of other animals is now guided by Allah ﷻ to do something noble. It buries another crow that was dead. Allah ﷻ humbles the humans with these lowly-seeming creatures especially when humans display arrogance. It is one of the recurring realities of Allah ﷻ referred to as sunnatullah that Allah ﷻ humbles or humiliates people with lowly-looking or frowned upon beings when people claim to have real authority, arrogance, and negative and unnecessary judgments. All of the judgments, if not guided, can lead to arrogance, backbiting, and the displeasure of Allah ﷻ. Then, the person becomes humiliated if he or she doesn't go back to Allah ﷻ by asking forgiveness from and making repentance to Allah ﷻ. As humans, our valuation systems can be messed up if we don't display humbleness and humility. May Allah ﷻ protect us, Amìn!

In addition, the crow is an accessible animal within almost all world habitats. The specific mention of the crow can also have significance especially in the realities of death which is the common shared reality for all existence.

Birds

There is the specific mention of the hoopoe (hud-hud) for the bird's ability to search and for its knowledge about Allah ﷻ. This can show an encouragement for humans to search for the people misguided by Shaytãn as mentioned[134] وَجَدتُّهَا وَقَوْمَهَا يَسْجُدُونَ لِلشَّمْسِ مِن دُونِ اللَّهِ وَزَيَّنَ لَهُمُ الشَّيْطَانُ أَعْمَالَهُمْ فَصَدَّهُمْ عَنِ السَّبِيلِ فَهُمْ لَا يَهْتَدُونَ {النمل/24}.

The key word وَجَدتُّهَا is repeated in the dialogue of hoopoe. In the previous ayah the same word is again emphasized with ta'kid إِنِّي وَجَدتُّ as[135]

إِنِّي وَجَدتُّ امْرَأَةً تَمْلِكُهُمْ وَأُوتِيَتْ مِن كُلِّ شَيْءٍ وَلَهَا عَرْشٌ عَظِيمٌ {النمل/23}. This can remind the person of the usûli principles of , من طلب وجد that whoever seeks, he or she finds. Finding the people who are misguided by Shaytãn is one of our responsibilities that is taught to us in the Qurãn by the hoopoe.

On the other hand, hoopoe teaches us a very critical theological point referred to as theodicy. Many people who are well-educated and who are worshipers of God can be misguided by Shaytãn if they don't understand this fine point. A bird understands but the humans do not understand. In the encounters of evil incidents such as misguidance, it is critical to not blame Allah ﷻ but to blame Shaytãn as mentioned وَزَيَّنَ لَهُمُ الشَّيْطَانُ أَعْمَالَهُمْ فَصَدَّهُمْ عَنِ السَّبِيلِ فَهُمْ لَا يَهْتَدُونَ {النمل/24}. Adab with Allah ﷻ requires always having good zann about Allah ﷻ. Allah ﷻ is Perfect and beyond humans' wrong renderings of imagination, blame, and negative constructions.

SubhanAllahi Rabbil Arshi Amma Yasifûn! [21:22], the Lord of the Throne, above that they describe!

Adab with teachers, parents, and good friends requires always having good zann about them although they may make mistakes. The primary adab is with Allah ﷻ. Then, adab with Rasulullah ﷺ and the sunnah of Rasulullah ﷺ follows. Then, the adab with parents and teachers and good friends follows.

---

134. I found her and her people prostrating to the sun instead of Allah ﷻ, and Satan has made their deeds pleasing to them and averted them from [His] way, so they are not guided,

135. Indeed, I found [there] a woman ruling them, and she has been given of all things, and she has a great throne.

When we analyze[136] لَأُعَذِّبَنَّهُ عَذَابًا شَدِيدًا أَوْ لَأَذْبَحَنَّهُ أَوْ لَيَأْتِيَنِّي بِسُلْطَانٍ مُّبِينٍ {النمل/21} فَمَكَثَ غَيْرَ بَعِيدٍ فَقَالَ أَحَطتُ بِمَا لَمْ تُحِطْ بِهِ وَجِئْتُكَ مِن سَبَإٍ بِنَبَإٍ يَقِينٍ {النمل/22} we can realize above mentioned sunnatullah. Sulayman as is a king. Kingship and authority require order and structure. In this regard, to establish and maintain the authority, there can be scary reminders of enforcement to remind the subjects of the outcomes of chaos as mentioned لَأُعَذِّبَنَّهُ عَذَابًا شَدِيدًا أَوْ لَأَذْبَحَنَّهُ. Yet, every rule can have an exception in a sound and healthy judgment system as mentioned أَوْ لَيَأْتِيَنِّي بِسُلْطَانٍ مُّبِينٍ.

Yet, sometimes we who are in the position of authority can be humbled by something or someone to remind us of our limits as mentioned أَحَطتُ بِمَا لَمْ تُحِطْ بِهِ وَجِئْتُكَ مِن سَبَإٍ بِنَبَإٍ يَقِينٍ {النمل/22}. In other words, we may hold authority in the family, in a group, in a town, in a school, or in a country with a reflected authority referred to as khalifah. Allah ﷻ holds the absolute Authority. All others hold the reflection of this Absolute Authority of Allah ﷻ as the khalifah of Allah ﷻ.

As a side note, everyone and everything speaks in its own language of habitat. Humans speak and understand within the social construct system of language in their habitat. The Qurãn primarily addresses humans and therefore the Qurãn uses a language that they would understand.

Birds view the world according to their understanding. They understand Divinity, Tawhid in Allah ﷻ in their own language. This is mentioned in[137] أَلَّا يَسْجُدُوا لِلَّهِ الَّذِي يُخْرِجُ الْخَبْءَ فِي السَّمَاوَاتِ وَالْأَرْضِ وَيَعْلَمُ مَا تُخْفُونَ وَمَا تُعْلِنُونَ {النمل/25} اللَّهُ لَا إِلَٰهَ إِلَّا هُوَ رَبُّ الْعَرْشِ الْعَظِيمِ {النمل/26}. The word الْخَبْءَ is a critical food item for the birds. By using its valuation system of importance for their sustenance (rizq), the hoopoe bird gives an example from an item that is so critical for the species of birds. Then, the bird very well and precisely explains the true Tawhid in Allah ﷻ. This is mentioned as اللَّهُ لَا إِلَٰهَ إِلَّا هُوَ رَبُّ الْعَرْشِ الْعَظِيمِ {النمل/26}. SubhanAllah!

---

136. 21. I will surely punish him with a severe punishment or slaughter him unless he brings me clear authorization."22. But the hoopoe stayed not long and said, "I have encompassed [in knowledge] that which you have not encompassed, and I have come to you from Sheba with certain news.

137. 25. [And] so they do not prostrate to Allah ﷻ, who brings forth what is hidden within the heavens and the earth and knows what you conceal and what you declare—26. Allah ﷻ—there is no deity except Him, Lord of the Great Throne."

[285-286][138]

آمَنَ الرَّسُولُ بِمَا أُنزِلَ إِلَيْهِ مِن رَّبِّهِ وَالْمُؤْمِنُونَ كُلٌّ آمَنَ بِاللّهِ وَمَلآئِكَتِهِ وَكُتُبِهِ وَرُسُلِهِ لاَ نُفَرِّقُ بَيْنَ أَحَدٍ مِّن رُّسُلِهِ وَقَالُواْ سَمِعْنَا وَأَطَعْنَا غُفْرَانَكَ رَبَّنَا وَإِلَيْكَ الْمَصِيرُ {البقرة/285} لاَ يُكَلِّفُ اللّهُ نَفْسًا إِلاَّ وُسْعَهَا لَهَا مَا كَسَبَتْ وَعَلَيْهَا مَا اكْتَسَبَتْ رَبَّنَا لاَ تُؤَاخِذْنَا إِن نَّسِينَا أَوْ أَخْطَأْنَا رَبَّنَا وَلاَ تَحْمِلْ عَلَيْنَا إِصْرًا كَمَا حَمَلْتَهُ عَلَى الَّذِينَ مِن قَبْلِنَا رَبَّنَا وَلاَ تُحَمِّلْنَا مَا لاَ طَاقَةَ لَنَا بِهِ وَاعْفُ عَنَّا وَاغْفِرْ لَنَا وَارْحَمْنَآ أَنتَ مَوْلاَنَا فَانصُرْنَا عَلَى الْقَوْمِ الْكَافِرِينَ {البقرة/286}

These two ayahs are suggested to be read after isha every day by Rasulullah 2] ﷺ] (hadith #4723) & [5] (hadith#807). There are very critical creed/aqãid-related parts in these verses. These verses also include dua, prayers teaching us how to make dua and ask for the best from Allah SWT. The teachings of these two ayahs also show the Mercy, Fadl and Rahmah of Allah ﷻ on this ummah.

To eliminate any type of doubt, waswasa and skepticism, it is important to be certain and to clearly show one's beliefs in the matters of religion.

In this sense, true religion is not a religion of humans. It is not generated by humans as some of the sociologists popularly used to view and understand religion as a product of social constructs of humanity.

True religion has the inductive and top-down approach of revelation. In this regard, Islãm is not generated by any human being including Rasulullah ﷺ, al-Habib ﷺ.

Therefore, the emphasis of آمَنَ الرَّسُولُ بِمَا أُنزِلَ إِلَيْهِ مِن رَّبِّهِ is very critical. The position of Rasulullah ﷺ and all of the prophets at the interface of communication with the Divine Transcendent Reality, Allah ﷻ through different means such as angels and other means shows that the true religion, Islãm, today or in the past as Nasara (Christianity), or Hûdan

138. 285. The Messenger has believed in what was revealed to him from his Lord, and [so have] the believers. All of them have believed in Allah ﷻ and His angels and His books and His messengers, [saying], "We make no distinction between any of His messengers." And they say, "We hear and we obey. [We seek] Your forgiveness, our Lord, and to You is the [final] destination."286. Allah ﷻ does not charge a soul except [with that within] its capacity. It will have [the consequence of] what [good] it has gained, and it will bear [the consequence of] what [evil] it has earned. "Our Lord, do not impose blame upon us if we have forgotten or erred. Our Lord, and lay not upon us a burden like that which You laid upon those before us. Our Lord, and burden us not with that which we have no ability to bear. And pardon us; and forgive us; and have mercy upon us. You are our protector, so give us victory over the disbelieving people."

(Judaism) always had the inductive approach of revelation. The true religion of Islãm has been revealed from Rabbul Alamin who has the Authority of[139] {الفاتحة/4} مَلِكِ يَوْمِ الدِّينِ.

Since it is a revelation and not a human invention or human construction, even the interface of this revelation called prophets or messengers have the position of believing and accepting what is revealed to them as mentioned with آمَنَ الرَّسُولُ بِمَا أُنزِلَ إِلَيْهِ مِن رَّبِّهِ. In other words, the prophets and messengers who are the blessed vehicles of these Transcendent Messages should firmly believe what is revealed to them from Rabbul Al'amin.

The blessed delivery and chosen position of the prophets as humans is repeatedly mentioned in the dialogue or conversations with their people or societies while they are relating the wahiy, revelation. For example,[140] قُلْ إِنَّمَا أَنَا بَشَرٌ مِّثْلُكُمْ يُوحَى إِلَيَّ أَنَّمَا إِلَهُكُمْ إِلَهٌ وَاحِدٌ فَمَن كَانَ يَرْجُو لِقَاء رَبِّهِ فَلْيَعْمَلْ عَمَلًا صَالِحًا وَلَا يُشْرِكْ بِعِبَادَةِ رَبِّهِ أَحَدًا {الكهف/110}

قُلْ إِنَّمَا أُنذِرُكُم بِالْوَحْيِ وَلَا يَسْمَعُ الصُّمُّ الدُّعَاء إِذَا مَا يُنذَرُونَ {الأنبياء/45}

قُلْ إِنَّمَا يُوحَى إِلَيَّ أَنَّمَا إِلَهُكُمْ إِلَهٌ وَاحِدٌ فَهَلْ أَنتُم مُّسْلِمُونَ {الأنبياء/108}

قُلْ إِنَّمَا أَنَا بَشَرٌ مِّثْلُكُمْ يُوحَى إِلَيَّ أَنَّمَا إِلَهُكُمْ إِلَهٌ وَاحِدٌ فَاسْتَقِيمُوا إِلَيْهِ وَاسْتَغْفِرُوهُ وَوَيْلٌ لِّلْمُشْرِكِينَ {فصلت/6}

One can realize in the above ayahs the emphasis on this blessed position of the prophets as humans being the ones who are delivering the message of Allah ﷻ to people with the expressions of قُلْ إِنَّمَا أَنَا بَشَرٌ مِّثْلُكُمْ قُلْ إِنَّمَا يُوحَى إِلَيَّ or قُلْ إِنَّمَا أُنذِرُكُم بِالْوَحْيِ or يُوحَى إِلَيَّ. Especially, the structure of يُوحَى إِلَيَّ in passive voice indicates that an action is done on the Fa'il, subject, with the External Divine Mashiyyah. The balagah and I'jãz of the Qurãn declares and announces this reality repeatedly with emphasis.

139. Sovereign of the Day of Recompense.

140. Kahf/110. Say, "I am only a man like you, to whom has been revealed that your god is one God. So whoever would hope for the meeting with his Lord—let him do righteous work and not associate in the worship of his Lord anyone." Anbiya/45. Say, "I only warn you by revelation." But the deaf do not hear the call when they are warned. Anbiya/108. Say, "It is only revealed to me that your god is but one God; so will you be Muslims [in submission to Him]?" Fusilat/6. Say, O [Muhammad ﷺ], "I am only a man like you to whom it has been revealed that your god is but one God; so take a straight course to Him and seek His forgiveness." And woe to those who associate others with Allah ﷻ -

If the prophets at the interface of the Divine Intersection of the wahiy, revelation have this disposition, then their followers also accept the inductive and top-down approach of the true religion, as mentioned with وَالْمُؤْمِنُونَ.

Now, one can ask, "Why is it top-down or inductive?"

The reason is because a person may not otherwise fully or correctly approach the realities of gayb for humans are more inclined to learn with the tools of deductive reasoning. Experimentation, trial & error methods, and positivism are all extensions of deductive reasoning more so in today's society and also in the past. In the realities of gayb, the acceptance of inductive reasoning called imãn, or belief is needed as mentioned كُلٌّ آمَنَ بِاللهِ وَمَلآئِكَتِهِ وَكُتُبِهِ وَرُسُلِهِ.

On another note, this is a pure attitude of reason beyond negative identity belongings. Therefore, a Muslim believes in all of the scriptures, books, and messages of the prophets sent by Allah ﷻ as mentioned لاَ نُفَرِّقُ بَيْنَ أَحَدٍ مِّن رُّسُلِهِ. There are no identity discussions of hasad, jealousy, or arrogance for a true Muslim when Allah ﷻ sends the same message at different times through different scriptures and prophets.

Inductive reality entails the acceptance of revelation. The reality of revelation entails the acceptance of imãn. Imãn requires the attitude of humbleness for the limited capacity of humans in knowledge, power, and ability. Humbleness requires submission and following as mentioned وَقَالُواْ سَمِعْنَا وَأَطَعْنَا.

Yet, most of our problems occur at the interface of inductive reason of وَقَالُواْ سَمِعْنَا وَأَطَعْنَا and deductive reasoning of 'it doesn't make sense', as mentioned in the categories of A and B.

A:[141]

قَالَ يَا إِبْلِيسُ مَا مَنَعَكَ أَن تَسْجُدَ لِمَا خَلَقْتُ بِيَدَيَّ أَسْتَكْبَرْتَ أَمْ كُنتَ مِنَ الْعَالِينَ {ص/75}
قَالَ أَنَا خَيْرٌ مِّنْهُ خَلَقْتَنِي مِن نَّارٍ وَخَلَقْتَهُ مِن طِينٍ {ص/76}

141. 75. [Allah ﷻ] said, "O Iblees, what prevented you from prostrating to that which I created with My hands? Were you arrogant [then], or were you [already] among the haughty?" 76. He said, "I am better than him. You created me from fire and created him from clay."

Or B:[142]

وَإِذْ قَالَ رَبُّكَ لِلْمَلاَئِكَةِ إِنِّي جَاعِلٌ فِي الأَرْضِ خَلِيفَةً قَالُواْ أَتَجْعَلُ فِيهَا مَن يُفْسِدُ فِيهَا
وَيَسْفِكُ الدِّمَاء وَنَحْنُ نُسَبِّحُ بِحَمْدِكَ وَنُقَدِّسُ لَكَ قَالَ إِنِّي أَعْلَمُ مَا لاَ تَعْلَمُونَ {البقرة/30}

The difference between the two categories of A and B is that the first category of A is the category of Shaytān who embodies the opposite of وَقَالُواْ سَمِعْنَا وَأَطَعْنَا and continues his disposition further with further arguments to show his embodiment of arrogance with this disposition as mentioned:[143]

قَالَ فَبِعِزَّتِكَ لَأُغْوِيَنَّهُمْ أَجْمَعِينَ {ص/82}

The second category B is the category of angels and some of the humans or jinn who embody وَقَالُواْ سَمِعْنَا وَأَطَعْنَا but sometimes make mistakes. It is similar to a stationary pendulum. Even though the pendulum may experience disturbance-just as a mistake causes temporary chaos- it ultimately comes back to its original, balanced position of equilibrium of sakina, and maintains this position as mentioned:[144]

قَالُواْ سُبْحَانَكَ لاَ عِلْمَ لَنَا إِلاَّ مَا عَلَّمْتَنَا إِنَّكَ أَنتَ الْعَلِيمُ الْحَكِيمُ {البقرة/32}

قَالاَ رَبَّنَا ظَلَمْنَا أَنفُسَنَا وَإِن لَّمْ تَغْفِرْ لَنَا وَتَرْحَمْنَا لَنَكُونَنَّ مِنَ الْخَاسِرِينَ {الأعراف/23}

Therefore, the second category of B should be our category to be in as mentioned in the ayah with the critical statement of[145] غُفْرَانَكَ رَبَّنَا وَإِلَيْكَ الْمَصِيرُ {البقرة/285}. In other words, if we make a mistake and lose our adab with Allah ,ﷻ then we immediately ask forgiveness from Rabbul A'lamìn accepting and remembering our limitations, weakness, and powerlessness. This is the real position of a Muslim.

142. And [mention, O Muhammad ﷺ], when your Lord said to the angels, "Indeed, I will make upon the earth a successive authority." They said, "Will You place upon it one who causes corruption therein and sheds blood, while we declare Your praise and sanctify You?" Allah ﷻ said, "Indeed, I know that which you do not know."

143. [Iblees] said, "By your might, I will surely mislead them all

144. Baqarah/32. They said, "Exalted are You; we have no knowledge except what You have taught us. Indeed, it is You who is the Knowing, the Wise." A'araf/23. They said, "Our Lord, we have wronged ourselves, and if You do not forgive us and have mercy upon us, we will surely be among the losers."

145. [We seek] Your forgiveness, our Lord, and to You is the [final] destination."

Then, the following ayah comes as[146] لَا يُكَلِّفُ اللّٰهُ نَفْسًا إِلاَّ وُسْعَهَا لَهَا مَا كَسَبَتْ وَعَلَيْهَا مَا اكْتَسَبَتْ رَبَّنَا لاَ تُؤَاخِذْنَا إِن نَّسِينَا أَوْ أَخْطَأْنَا رَبَّنَا وَلاَ تَحْمِلْ عَلَيْنَا إِصْرًا كَمَا حَمَلْتَهُ عَلَى الَّذِينَ مِن قَبْلِنَا رَبَّنَا وَلاَ تُحَمِّلْنَا مَا لاَ طَاقَةَ لَنَا بِهِ وَاعْفُ عَنَّا وَاغْفِرْ لَنَا وَارْحَمْنَآ أَنتَ مَوْلاَنَا فَانصُرْنَا عَلَى الْقَوْمِ الْكَافِرِينَ. {البقرة/286}

This ayah assures the humble position of the person with true imãn making an invitation and begging constantly for the Fadl, Rahmah and Mercy of Allah ﷻ. The request from Allah ﷻ is that Allah ﷻ makes life easy for us and gives us endurance against the trials and tests. We have our weakness and lack of self-control. Yet, we fully trust in and submit to Allah ﷻ that Allah ﷻ will forgive us although we may have a lot of shortcomings. We don't trust the outcome of our own actions but trust in Allah ﷻ and expect all of the outcomes from Allah ﷻ as mentioned أَنتَ مَوْلاَنَا.

This is the opposite case of Shaytãn and his followers claiming self-sufficiency, independence, and assurance in trusting the outcome of their own actions. In this sense, the pronoun 'I' with the takid as لَأُغْوِيَنَّهُمْ in[147] {ص/82} قَالَ فَبِعِزَّتِكَ لَأُغْوِيَنَّهُمْ أَجْمَعِينَ is interesting. It can indicate the display of trusting one's own actions but not trusting in Allah ﷻ. May Allah ﷻ protect us, Amìn!

Yet, sometimes Allah ﷻ lets a zãlim make a change in a society. As mentioned in the hadith, Azzãlimu sayfu Allah, [17]. Or, another hadith mentions that Allah ﷻ raises the religion onto the shoulders of a fãsiq [17].

The above ahadith all show that Allah ﷻ is in Full Control and Authority although the apparent incidents may appear to be destructive and pessimistic. Yet, in many of the ayahs of the Qurãn this is mentioned, for example, to be similar as:[148]

---

146. Allah ﷻ does not charge a soul except [with that within] its capacity. It will have [the consequence of] what [good] it has gained, and it will bear [the consequence of] what [evil] it has earned. "Our Lord, do not impose blame upon us if we have forgotten or erred. Our Lord, and lay not upon us a burden like that which You laid upon those before us. Our Lord, and burden us not with that which we have no ability to bear. And pardon us; and forgive us; and have mercy upon us. You are our protector, so give us victory over the disbelieving people."
147. [Iblees] said, "By your might, I will surely mislead them all
148. Naml/50. And they planned a plan, and We planned a plan, while they perceived not. Al-Imran/54. And the disbelievers planned, but Allah ﷻ planned. And Allah ﷻ is the best of planners. Al-Anfal/30. And [remember, O Muhammad ﷺ], when those who disbelieved plotted against you to restrain you or kill you or evict you [from Makkah]. But they plan, and Allah plans. And Allah ﷻ is the best of planners.

وَمَكَرُوا مَكْرًا وَمَكَرْنَا مَكْرًا وَهُمْ لَا يَشْعُرُونَ {النمل/50}

وَمَكَرُواْ وَمَكَرَ اللهُ وَاللهُ خَيْرُ الْمَاكِرِينَ {آل عمران/54}

وَإِذْ يَمْكُرُ بِكَ الَّذِينَ كَفَرُواْ لِيُثْبِتُوكَ أَوْ يَقْتُلُوكَ أَوْ يُخْرِجُوكَ وَيَمْكُرُونَ وَيَمْكُرُ اللهُ وَاللهُ خَيْرُ الْمَاكِرِينَ {الأنفال/30}

Similarly, Shaytãn mentions as[149] قَالَ فَبِعِزَّتِكَ لَأُغْوِيَنَّهُمْ أَجْمَعِينَ {ص/82} إِلاَّ عِبَادَكَ مِنْهُمُ الْمُخْلَصِينَ {ص/83}. Allah ﷻ mentions this reality as قَالَ فَالْحَقُّ وَالْحَقَّ أَقُولُ {ص/84} that Allah ﷻ gives allowance and an apparent enablement for Shaytãn as mentioned[150] قَالَ رَبِّ فَأَنظِرْنِي إِلَى يَوْمِ يُبْعَثُونَ {ص/79} قَالَ فَإِنَّكَ مِنَ الْمُنظَرِينَ {ص/80}. Shaytãn may think that he is proving himself as mentioned قَالَ فَبِعِزَّتِكَ لَأُغْوِيَنَّهُمْ أَجْمَعِينَ {ص/82} إِلَّا عِبَادَكَ مِنْهُمُ.

Yet, Remember!

Allah ﷻ raises and elevates this deen, Islãm, onto the shoulders of a zãlim and fãsiq sometimes to differentiate the dirt from the purity. This zãlim and fãsiq can be Shaytãn or his followers at any time or in any place. Yet, they are just sabab, apparent reasons for the purification process.

Yet, all the zãlim and fãsiq will get their punishments according to their intentions as mentioned[151] لَأَمْلَأَنَّ جَهَنَّمَ مِنكَ وَمِمَّن تَبِعَكَ مِنْهُمْ أَجْمَعِينَ {ص/85}.

In other words, a zãlim or a fãsiq cannot claim that their evil-intended actions turned into a good result. Therefore, they should receive rewards. This is a fallacy.

Rasulullah ﷺ mentions that "Innamal a'malum binniyah." Everything is according to its intention [4].

---

149. 82. [Iblees] said, "By your might, I will surely mislead them all 83. Except, among them, Your chosen servants." 84. [Allah ﷻ] said, "The truth [is My oath], and the truth I say -

150. 79. He said, "My Lord, then reprieve me until the Day they are resurrected." 80. [Allah ﷻ] said, "So indeed, you are of those reprieved 82. [Iblees] said, "By your might, I will surely mislead them all

151. [That] I will surely fill Hell with you and those of them that follow you all together."

Sûrah 3 – ãl ìmrãn

[159][152]

فَبِمَا رَحْمَةٍ مِّنَ اللّهِ لِنتَ لَهُمْ وَلَوْ كُنتَ فَظًّا غَلِيظَ الْقَلْبِ لاَنفَضُّواْ مِنْ حَوْلِكَ فَاعْفُ عَنْهُمْ وَاسْتَغْفِرْ لَهُمْ وَشَاوِرْهُمْ فِي الأَمْرِ فَإِذَا عَزَمْتَ فَتَوَكَّلْ عَلَى اللّهِ إِنَّ اللّهَ يُحِبُّ الْمُتَوَكِّلِينَ {آل عمران/159}

In speaking and delivery of the message, softness and not harshness is important. Most of the time, harshness, rudeness, and anger can entail and indicate arrogance.

Most of the time, harshness, rudeness, and anger break the hearts regardless of whether or not the person is telling the truth.

Most of the time, softness, kindness, and gentleness win the hearts regardless of whether or not the person is telling the truth.

Therefore, today, there is a lot of dalalah, misguidance which is delivered through methods of softness, kindness, and gentleness and misguides the people and Muslims. May Allah ﷻ protect us and give us the ability, heart, forbearance, and character of softness, gentleness, and kindness in our uslûb of delivery of the message and communication at all levels, Amìn.

One can review the dire need of this uslûb especially among the brothers, sisters, family, and Muslims as mentioned[153] رُحَمَاء بَيْنَهُمْ in مُّحَمَّدٌ رَّسُولُ اللَّهِ وَالَّذِينَ مَعَهُ أَشِدَّاء عَلَى الْكُفَّارِ رُحَمَاء بَيْنَهُمْ تَرَاهُمْ رُكَّعًا سُجَّدًا يَبْتَغُونَ فَضْلًا مِّنَ اللَّهِ وَرِضْوَانًا سِيمَاهُمْ فِي وُجُوهِهِم مِّنْ أَثَرِ السُّجُودِ ذَلِكَ مَثَلُهُمْ فِي التَّوْرَاةِ وَمَثَلُهُمْ فِي الْإِنجِيلِ كَزَرْعٍ أَخْرَجَ شَطْأَهُ فَآزَرَهُ فَاسْتَغْلَظَ فَاسْتَوَى عَلَى سُوقِهِ يُعْجِبُ الزُّرَّاعَ لِيَغِيظَ بِهِمُ الْكُفَّارَ وَعَدَ اللَّهُ الَّذِينَ آمَنُوا وَعَمِلُوا الصَّالِحَاتِ مِنْهُم مَّغْفِرَةً وَأَجْرًا عَظِيمًا {الفتح/92}.

One can realize the dire need of this uslûb especially for the authority holders in a family. For example, the father is the authority holder and

---

152. So by mercy from Allah ﷻ, [O Muhammad ﷺ], you were lenient with them. And if you had been rude [in speech] and harsh in heart, they would have disbanded from about you. So pardon them and ask forgiveness for them and consult them in the matter. And when you have decided, then rely upon Allah. Indeed, Allah ﷻ loves those who rely [upon Him].

153. Muhammad ﷺ is the Messenger of Allah; and those with him are forceful against the disbelievers, merciful among themselves. You see them bowing and prostrating [in prayer], seeking bounty from Allah ﷻ and [His] pleasure. Their mark is on their faces from the trace of prostration. That is their description in the Torah. And their description in the Gospel is as a plant which produces its offshoots and strengthens them so they grow firm and stand upon their stalks, delighting the sowers—so that Allah ﷻ may enrage by them the disbelievers. Allah ﷻ has promised those who believe and do righteous deeds among them forgiveness and a great reward.

the child is the follower depicted in the following ayahs. Yet, the father uses such a gentle, loving, and caring uslûb as يَا بُنَيَّ repeatedly in[154]

يَا بُنَيَّ إِنَّهَا إِن تَكُ مِثْقَالَ حَبَّةٍ مِّنْ خَرْدَلٍ فَتَكُن فِي صَخْرَةٍ أَوْ فِي السَّمَاوَاتِ أَوْ فِي الْأَرْضِ يَأْتِ بِهَا اللَّهُ إِنَّ اللَّهَ لَطِيفٌ خَبِيرٌ {لقمان/16} يَا بُنَيَّ أَقِمِ الصَّلَاةَ وَأْمُرْ بِالْمَعْرُوفِ وَانْهَ عَنِ الْمُنكَرِ وَاصْبِرْ عَلَى مَا أَصَابَكَ إِنَّ ذَلِكَ مِنْ عَزْمِ الْأُمُورِ {لقمان/17}

One should remember that when someone holds the authority and yet does not execute the power of this authority at the times when reprimand is needed, but rather reminds the person with kindness, then these can be critical moments and turning points for affecting the person. At such times, one can gain and have the true love, respect, and admiration for the authority holder.

In its true and absolute sense, we deserve at each second and all of the time reprimands due to our belligerent and non-adab relationship with Allah ﷻ. Yet, Allah ﷻ gives us time. Allah ﷻ reminds us and always gives us kind and gentle advice as repeated in Sûrah Fatiha as[155] الْحَمْدُ لِلَّهِ رَبِّ الْعَالَمِينَ {الفاتحة/2} الرَّحْمنِ الرَّحِيمِ {الفاتحة/3} مَلِكِ يَوْمِ الدِّينِ {الفاتحة/4}. As one can realize the expressions رَبِّ الْعَالَمِينَ {الفاتحة/2} and مَلِكِ يَوْمِ الدِّينِ {الفاتحة/4} are constant reminders for us of the Absolute, the True and the Real Authority of Allah ﷻ. Yet, Allah ﷻ reminds us that Allah ﷻ is the Most Merciful, the Most Caring, the Most Gentle, the Most Loving and the Most Kind with the repetitions of[156], الرَّحْمنِ الرَّحِيمِ {الفاتحة/3} and بِسْمِ اللهِ الرَّحْمَنِ الرَّحِيمِ {الفاتحة/1}. Moreover, the word رَبِّ is repeated constantly in the Qurân to emphasize that Allah ﷻ is the Most Merciful, the Most Caring, the Most Gentle, the Most Loving.

One can review and understand in all of the above perspectives that harshness, anger, rudeness, raising of the voice, complaining without any purpose, always criticizing without any purpose, and not appreciating or thanking are all destructive behaviors. Even facial expressions in the form of a bad look, frowning rather than making a pleasant face, will always be detrimental and harmful especially for humans who always like to cross the boundaries of adab. Therefore, let's adopt niceness and

154. O my son, establish prayer, enjoin what is right, forbid what is wrong, and be patient over what befalls you. Indeed, [all] that is of the matters [requiring] determination.

155. 2. [All] praise is [due] to Allah ﷻ, Lord of the worlds—3. The Entirely Merciful, the Especially Merciful, 4. Sovereign of the Day of Recompense.

156. 1. In the name of Allah ﷻ, the Entirely Merciful, the Especially Merciful. 3. The Entirely Merciful, the Especially Merciful,

struggle for it and ask from Allah ﷻ the Tawfiq with the Divine Fadl and Grace.

Allahumma Ja'alna attibu' khuliqi Rasulullah ﷺ, Habibuka, Amìn اللهم جعلنا اتبع خلقي رسول الله صلى الله عليه وسلم ، حبيبك، آمين

Allahumma La takilni nafsan tarfata a'ynin, Amìn اللهم لا تكلني نفسا طرفة عين

Allahumma Tahhir Qulubuna min al-fawãhish, Amìn اللهم طهر قلوبنا من الفواحش ، آمين

Allahumma thabit Qulubuna al'a qawli layyin, uslûbu layyin, sawtu layyin, nazaru layyin, misla Habibuka, al-Mustafa ﷺ, Amìn اللهم ثبت قلوبنا على قول لين،اصلب لين،صوت لين ،نظر لين، مثل حبيبك، ،المصطفى صلى الله عليه وسلم ، آمين

Allahumma nahnu dua'fu, fansurna ala anfusina, fansurna ala a'daina, fansurna ala qawmil kafirin, wal munafiqin, wal fasiqin min al Jinn wal ins, Amì اللهم نحن ضعفاء ، فانصرنا على انفسنا ،فانصرنا على اعداءنا ، فانصرنا على قوم كافرين ، والمنافقين، والفاسقين من الجن والانس، آمين

Allahumma Inna Zalamna anfusuna fain tagfirrlana watakanna min al khasirin, Amìn اللهم انا ظلمنا انفسنا فان تغفرلنا وتقعنا من الخاسرين ، آمين

Wa la hawla wala quwwata illa billahil Alayil Azim, Amìn و لا حول و لا قوة إلا بالله العلى العظيم، آمين

Walhamdu lillahi Rabbil Alamin, Amìn و الحمد لله رب العالمين

Allahumma Salli ala Sayyidina wa Habibina Muhammad, al-Mustafa, bi hurmati Taha, Yasin, Amìn اللهم صلى على سيدنا و حبيبنا محمد المصطفى ، بحرمت طه،يس، آمين.

[190-194][157]

إِنَّ فِي خَلْقِ السَّمَاوَاتِ وَالأَرْضِ وَاخْتِلاَفِ اللَّيْلِ وَالنَّهَارِ لآيَاتٍ لِّأُوْلِي الألْبَابِ {آل
عمران/190} الَّذِينَ يَذْكُرُونَ اللّهَ قِيَامًا وَقُعُودًا وَعَلَىَ جُنُوبِهِمْ وَيَتَفَكَّرُونَ فِي خَلْقِ
السَّمَاوَاتِ وَالأَرْضِ رَبَّنَا مَا خَلَقْتَ هَذا بَاطِلاً سُبْحَانَكَ فَقِنَا عَذَابَ النَّارِ {آل عمران/191}
رَبَّنَا إِنَّكَ مَن تُدْخِلِ النَّارَ فَقَدْ أَخْزَيْتَهُ وَمَا لِلظَّالِمِينَ مِنْ أَنصَارٍ {آل عمران/192} رَّبَّنَا
إِنَّنَا سَمِعْنَا مُنَادِيًا يُنَادِي لِلإِيمَانِ أَنْ آمِنُواْ بِرَبِّكُمْ فَآمَنَّا رَبَّنَا فَاغْفِرْ لَنَا ذُنُوبَنَا وَكَفِّرْ عَنَّا
سَيِّئَاتِنَا وَتَوَفَّنَا مَعَ الأبْرَارِ {آل عمران/193} رَبَّنَا وَآتِنَا مَا وَعَدتَّنَا عَلَى رُسُلِكَ وَلاَ تُخْزِنَا
يَوْمَ الْقِيَامَةِ إِنَّكَ لاَ تُخْلِفُ الْمِيعَادَ {آل عمران/194}

One should really critically analyze what and why Rasulullah ﷺ, al-Habib did as the sunnah for the ummah. Above is a passage from the Qurãn that Rasulullah ﷺ, al-Mustafa used to read when he woke up at night while observing and looking at the stars in the sky. Today, how many of us are connected to nature and the creation in their real purpose of existence through the teachings of the Qurãn and the sunnah?

Rasulullah ﷺ shows us a practical example of applying the teachings of the Qurãn in the encounters of night and in the observation of stars with astonishment, awe, and pleasure connecting nature to its real purpose of creation as mentioned رَبَّنَا مَا خَلَقْتَ هَذا بَاطِلاً.

Purposelessness is a disease in one's life. Attributing purposelessness to the creation and to nature is another continuation and projection of this initial disease of having no purpose or false purpose.

If one has a real and true purpose in life, then he or she can find all of the true and real purpose of the creation with the Fadl and Rahmah of Allah ﷻ.

One should always remember to embody SubhanAllah in order to negate our own and other's false attributions to the creation and the

157. 190. Indeed, in the creation of the heavens and the earth and the alternation of the night and the day are signs for those of understanding 191. Who remember Allah ﷻ while standing or sitting or [lying] on their sides and give thought to the creation of the heavens and the earth, [saying], "Our Lord, You did not create this aimlessly; exalted are You [above such a thing]; then protect us from the punishment of the Fire. 192. Our Lord, indeed whoever You admit to the Fire—You have disgraced him, and for the wrongdoers there are no helpers. 193. Our Lord, indeed we have heard a caller calling to faith, [saying], 'Believe in your Lord,' and we have believed. Our Lord, so forgive us our sins and remove from us our misdeeds and cause us to die with the righteous. 194 Our Lord, and grant us what You promised us through Your messengers and do not disgrace us on the Day of Resurrection. Indeed, You do not fail in [Your] promise."

universe in their true, real, and absolute relationship with Allah ﷻ. This is mentioned with the phrase سُبْحَانَكَ in رَبَّنَا مَا خَلَقْتَ هَذا بَاطِلاً سُبْحَانَكَ.

Rasulullah ﷺ teaches us a personal trait. After observing nature, the stars, and the universe, one should ask for forgiveness and protection from the punishment of Allah ﷻ due to our possible unappreciative behaviors towards all different creations regarding their real purpose and goal. This dua is:[158]

رَبَّنَا إِنَّكَ مَن تُدْخِلِ النَّارَ فَقَدْ أَخْزَيْتَهُ وَمَا لِلظَّالِمِينَ مِنْ أَنصَارٍ {آل عمران/192} رَّبَّنَا إِنَّنَا سَمِعْنَا مُنَادِيًا يُنَادِي لِلإِيمَانِ أَنْ آمِنُواْ بِرَبِّكُمْ فَآمَنَّا رَبَّنَا فَاغْفِرْ لَنَا ذُنُوبَنَا وَكَفِّرْ عَنَّا سَيِّئَاتِنَا وَتَوَفَّنَا مَعَ الأبْرَارِ {آل عمران/193} رَبَّنَا وَآتِنَا مَا وَعَدتَّنَا عَلَى رُسُلِكَ وَلاَ تُخْزِنَا يَوْمَ الْقِيَامَةِ إِنَّكَ لاَ تُخْلِفُ الْمِيعَادَ {آل عمران/194}

Juz 9

Sûrah 8 al-Anfãl

[25][159]

وَاتَّقُواْ فِتْنَةً لاَّ تُصِيبَنَّ الَّذِينَ ظَلَمُواْ مِنكُمْ خَآصَّةً وَاعْلَمُواْ أَنَّ اللّهَ شَدِيدُ الْعِقَابِ {الأنفال/25}

When we analyze this ayah with other ayahs of the Qurãn and various ahadith of Rasulullah ﷺ, then one can realize a few critical points on practical stances during the times of conflict, abuse, and oppression:

When there is social chaos, one should not be part of it.

A Muslim should not increase the existing chaos or conflicts by any means.

A Muslim should not be on the side of the oppressor and abuser.

158. 192. Our Lord, indeed whoever You admit to the Fire—You have disgraced him, and for the wrongdoers there are no helpers. 193. Our Lord, indeed we have heard a caller calling to faith, [saying], 'Believe in your Lord,' and we have believed. Our Lord, so forgive us our sins and remove from us our misdeeds and cause us to die with the righteous. 194. Our Lord, and grant us what You promised us through Your messengers and do not disgrace us on the Day of Resurrection. Indeed, You do not fail in [Your] promise."

159. And fear a trial which will not strike those who have wronged among you exclusively, and know that Allah is severe in penalty.

Not being on the side of the oppressor and abuser does not necessarily mean fighting against them physically and verbally if there is escalating chaos that can lead to the killings of many people.

The practical avoidance of chaos or conflict can entail a passive stance with active patience and sincere dua, prayer to Allah ﷻ for the removal of the chaos and conflicts.

The passive stance can mean and indicate staying at home, not joining in the physical demonstrations, locking the doors, shutting the TV off, and other communication devices in order to not be affected and disturbed.

The passive stance can indicate leaving one's belongings, house, residence, and wealth and migrating to another town, city, or country when and if necessary.

If global chaos occurs, the passive stance can indicate moving to places of isolation such as farms, valleys, and mountains to promote one's survival and minimize human interaction.

The passive stance can require not defending oneself if the oppressor attacks the person during times of social chaos and fitnah.

The above points can be present especially during times of social chaos. The conflicts among individuals should be handled differently than what is mentioned in the above steps. Here we are not talking here about the cases of abuse, oppression, or conflicts between the spouses in a marriage or other types of chaos experienced between individuals.

The above bulleted points can be some steps during the times or on the verge of social chaos, when there are angry masses that can be motivated, instigated, and provoked easily. The protestors can potentially engage themselves with vandalism, killing others, and destruction of personal, civil, and public properties. In these engagements, there can be a flow of anger to drag everyone into this movement to destroy, kill, and vandalize when it can potentially become a mass action. In these types of social flow, the individuals may not be aware of why they are protesting. This type of chaos is worse than killing as mentioned in the Qurãn [2:191]. One can vividly remember the results of Syrian, Yemeni, and Egyptian chaos and turmoil resulting in the killings of millions with the so-called hashtag of 'Arab Spring'.

A sound-minded individual should always check and balance his or her initial reason of involvement to see if the initial goal still matches the current means of achieving this goal. If the person did not care in the beginning about killing, stealing, and destroying, then this in itself can be an evil start covered with another costume. If the person did start with a good intention of seeking justice and if he or she sees any problem within a mass movement causing evil results in the pursuit of achieving this goal, then he or she should immediately stop and follow the above bulleted steps.

Allahu A'lam. الله اعلم

Allahumma Ajirna Min al-Fithnah, Amìn! اللهم اجرنا من الفتنه، آمين

Juz 10

Sûrah 8 al-Anfãl

[46][160]

وَأَطِيعُواْ اللّهَ وَرَسُولَهُ وَلاَ تَنَازَعُواْ فَتَفْشَلُواْ وَتَذْهَبَ رِيحُكُمْ وَاصْبِرُواْ إِنَّ اللّهَ مَعَ الصَّابِرِينَ {الأنفال/46}

Victories & Openings after Being Patient

It is very difficult to not argue. Especially, when we live during a time when generating conflict is understood to be a virtue rather than a problem. Argumentation, confrontation, and questioning for the sake of questioning are the approaches of the modern society. Even, this attitude went in such an extreme, so out of control, that one can find books in popular media especially in the West titled as "Arguing with God", astagfirullah, SubhanAllah amma yushriqûn.

This is the full loss of adab. The people are so very disconnected with the notions of adab, but filled with the notions of arrogance embodying the 'ana', 'I', 'me' or 'myself'. Unfortunately, in a globalized society with internet and others, Muslims are deeply and greatly being affected by these diseases. Yet, by titles they can still be Muslims, and Allah ﷻ knows all of our essences. May Allah ﷻ protect us from misguidance, Amìn!

In one of my ethnographic works with Yemeni communities [18], one of the imams made a comment saying, "Today's Muslims are worse than the pre-Islamic Arabs in morality and ethics." It was shocking for me to hear that from someone who is Arab and from Yemen where the

160. And obey Allah ﷻ and His Messenger, and do not dispute and [thus] lose courage and [then] your strength would depart; and be patient. Indeed, Allah ﷻ is with the patient.

genuine teachings are still practiced in nomadic or Bedouin society. Yet, he was alluding to the widespread notions of ethical problems such as bribery, cheating, lying, using the religion with politics and not hesitating to amplify the personal and social conflicts in lieu of personal gain in Muslim societies. Although I disagreed with him in that we cannot generalize this statement, yet, one can question the essence of Islãm today and how it is practiced and understood today compared to the time of Rasulullah ﷺ and earlier salaf. May Allah ﷻ help us follow the sunnah of Rasulullah ﷺ, Amìn!

Although critical thinking and questioning with adab to understand in order to change one's position is a virtue, our point is the problem of the increasing trends in lifestyles promoting individualization in modern societies that break any type of bonds including family bonds, parent-child bonds, husband-wife bonds, and others. This is a social effect as an external agent shaping the individual with expected norms in the society.

Another perspective of difficulty arises intrinsically when the person holds the nafs or raw ego as the nafs-ammara which does not like to follow, does not like to take orders, and does not like to submit but has the inclinations of opposition, confrontation, and shows the inclinations toward arrogance. This is the intrinsic perspective of an internal agent shaping the individual with its tendencies.

In both internal and external perspectives, there are the effects of Shaytãn amplifying this chaos and disunity among the individuals, families, friends, and in the societies.

With all of these different challenges, if the person still bears with patience and does not join the general club of 'people with problems', the person can have great openings of khayr to please Allah ﷻ in his or her life. In other words, Allah ﷻ can give a lot of enablement, barakah, and achievements to this person with the Divine Fadl and Rahmah.

The reason for these great openings is that it is very difficult to not be angry and to maintain patience with composure, and to not fight or argue in different relationships. These relationships can be between the husband and wife, children and parents, and in other relationships.

On the other hand, when we analyze the life of Rasulullah ,ﷺ his life ﷺ gives an example of how one can achieve and overcome these difficulties.[161]

لَقَدْ جَاءكُمْ رَسُولٌ مِّنْ أَنفُسِكُمْ عَزِيزٌ عَلَيْهِ مَا عَنِتُّمْ حَرِيصٌ عَلَيْكُم بِالْمُؤْمِنِينَ رَؤُوفٌ رَّحِيمٌ {التوبة/128} فَإِن تَوَلَّوْاْ فَقُلْ حَسْبِيَ اللّهُ لا إِلَهَ إِلاَّ هُوَ عَلَيْهِ تَوَكَّلْتُ وَهُوَ رَبُّ الْعَرْشِ الْعَظِيمِ {التوبة/129}

فَبِمَا رَحْمَةٍ مِّنَ اللّهِ لِنتَ لَهُمْ وَلَوْ كُنتَ فَظًّا غَلِيظَ الْقَلْبِ لاَنفَضُّواْ مِنْ حَوْلِكَ فَاعْفُ عَنْهُمْ وَاسْتَغْفِرْ لَهُمْ وَشَاوِرْهُمْ فِي الأَمْرِ فَإِذَا عَزَمْتَ فَتَوَكَّلْ عَلَى اللّهِ إِنَّ اللّهَ يُحِبُّ الْمُتَوَكِّلِينَ {آل عمران/159}[162]

One should recognize that Rasulullah ﷺ is a special creation of Allah ﷻ as mentioned فَبِمَا رَحْمَةٍ مِّنَ اللّهِ. Rasulullah ﷺ is رَؤُوفٌ رَّحِيمٌ. Rasulullah is not an ordinary human being. He ﷺ is special, elected, elevated, and peaked in different parts of u'budiyyah of Allah ﷻ.

One of the charming features of Rasulullah ﷺ is لِنتَ لَهُمْ. This is being layyinah, having a soft, gentle, empathetic, caring, pleasant, and loving character. During incidents when a normal or a pious person or a waliyy of Allah ﷻ can possibly or for sure lose control of himself or herself, Rasulullah ﷺ still maintains layyinah, calmness, composure, and fully pleasant attributes.

On the other hand, one should remember that at the end of these self-struggles of cleansing the heart from the spiritual diseases of hasad, and being patient, there may be still remnants of these diseases before one dies and failed outcomes of not being patient. With the Grace and Fadl of Allah ,ﷻ Allah ﷻ can remove them as mentioned[163] وَنَزَعْنَا مَا فِي صُدُورِهِم مِّنْ غِلٍّ إِخْوَانًا عَلَى سُرُرٍ مُّتَقَابِلِينَ {الحجر/47}. This can be due to the constant and unending struggle of the person with oneself to embody patience and the character of layyinah similar to Rasulullah ﷺ.

---

161. 128. There has certainly come to you a Messenger from among yourselves. Grievous to him is what you suffer; [he is] concerned over you and to the believers is kind and merciful. 129. But if they turn away, [O Muhammad ﷺ], say, "Sufficient for me is Allah ﷻ; there is no deity except Him. On Him I have relied, and He is the Lord of the Great Throne."

162. So by mercy from Allah ﷻ , [O Muhammad ﷺ], you were lenient with them. And if you had been rude [in speech] and harsh in heart, they would have disbanded from about you. So pardon them and ask forgiveness for them and consult them in the matter. And when you have decided, then rely upon Allah. Indeed, Allah ﷻ loves those who rely [upon Him].

163. And We will remove whatever is in their breasts of resentment, [so they will be] brothers, on thrones facing each other.

It is very critical to ask for patience and embodiment of the character of being layyinah from Allah ﷻ as this character was also given to Rasulullah ﷺ by Allah ﷻ as mentioned فَبِمَا رَحْمَةٍ مِّنَ اللهِ.

If Allah ﷻ does not give it to the person, even if the person goes to the best psychologist or counselors in the world, the person will still be harsh and lose oneself in easy or difficult challenges of life.

Each stored potential energy in a person due to the unjust behaviors of others can have an opening for the person as mentioned in the hadith that Allah ﷻ is with the ones who are oppressed and who have broken hearts [2] (hadith# 4090).

Here, the struggle of the person towards the removal of these diseases is the key. Therefore, Allah ﷻ can show the Divine Fadl and Grace to remove them so that they can enter the Jannah if there is the intention and struggle of removing these diseases as mentioned وَنَزَعْنَا مَا فِي صُدُورِهِم مِّنْ غِلٍّ إِخْوَانً.

One should first recognize and accept one's spiritual problems to move on to the next step of removal.

Allahumma La Takilni Nafsan Tarfata A'yunin! اللهم لا تكلنى نفساً طرفت عيونٍ

Oh Allah ! Do not leave us with our own selves for even less than a second!

Oh Allah ! We can not do without You.

Oh Allah ! Please make us have the character of layyinah similar to Rasulullah ﷺ!

Amìn, bi hurmati and shafa'ati Habibuka, Rasulullah ﷺ. آمين بحرمت و شفاعة حبيبك، رسول الله صلى الله عليه وسلم

Juz 13

Sûrah 12- Yûsuf

[53][164]

وَمَا أُبَرِّىءُ نَفْسِي إِنَّ النَّفْسَ لأَمَّارَةٌ بِالسُّوءِ إِلاَّ مَا رَحِمَ رَبِّيَ إِنَّ رَبِّي غَفُورٌ رَّحِيمٌ
{يوسف/53}

164. And I do not acquit myself. Indeed, the soul is a persistent enjoiner of evil, except those upon which my Lord has mercy. Indeed, my Lord is Forgiving and Merciful."

Sometimes, when we are blamed for something, there can be different dispositions by awliyaullah.

One disposition is that the blamed awliya does not say or do anything about it and remains silent. He or she just moves on even though he or she knows that he or she is innocent. The person did not really deserve the blame. This level of awliya is very high and requires a lot of patience, tawakkul, taslim, and tawfidh. In this regard, the person does not want to expose this secret that he or she was blamed and keeps this secret until one dies and expects the reward for it from Allah ﷻ.

Although modern psychology can call this trauma defined as 'a deeply distressing or disturbing experience', [2] the people of Allah ﷻ referred to as awliyaullah, welcome everything as a guest from Allah ﷻ. Among these guests, there can be blame on a person, evil-seeming incidents, trials. and tests. The person of Allah ﷻ always keeps silent in order to not displease Allah ﷻ by increasing the possibilities of fitnah while exposing the faults of others.

This state is very high. One of the elect individuals who embodied this state is Rasulullah .ﷺ There were a lot of incidents in the life of Rasulullah ﷺ that he ﷺ kept secret in himself with full reliance and tawakkul on Allah .ﷻ Allah ,ﷻ as the N'imal Mawla wa N'imal Wakìl protected al-ḥabib .ﷺ Here is an example of this in the interaction of Rasulullah ﷺ with the women similar to the case of the content of the case of Yusuf as with the women:[165]

وَإِذْ أَسَرَّ النَّبِيُّ إِلَى بَعْضِ أَزْوَاجِهِ حَدِيثًا فَلَمَّا نَبَّأَتْ بِهِ وَأَظْهَرَهُ اللَّهُ عَلَيْهِ عَرَّفَ بَعْضَهُ وَأَعْرَضَ عَن بَعْضٍ فَلَمَّا نَبَّأَهَا بِهِ قَالَتْ مَنْ أَنبَأَكَ هَٰذَا قَالَ نَبَّأَنِيَ الْعَلِيمُ الْخَبِيرُ {التحريم/3} إِن تَتُوبَا إِلَى اللَّهِ فَقَدْ صَغَتْ قُلُوبُكُمَا وَإِن تَظَاهَرَا عَلَيْهِ فَإِنَّ اللَّهَ هُوَ مَوْلَاهُ وَجِبْرِيلُ وَصَالِحُ الْمُؤْمِنِينَ وَالْمَلَائِكَةُ بَعْدَ ذَٰلِكَ ظَهِيرٌ {التحريم/4} عَسَىٰ رَبُّهُ إِن طَلَّقَكُنَّ أَن يُبْدِلَهُ أَزْوَاجًا خَيْرًا مِّنكُنَّ مُسْلِمَاتٍ مُّؤْمِنَاتٍ قَانِتَاتٍ تَائِبَاتٍ عَابِدَاتٍ سَائِحَاتٍ ثَيِّبَاتٍ وَأَبْكَارًا {التحريم/5}

165. 3. And [remember] when the Prophet confided to one of his wives a statement; and when she informed [another] of it and Allah showed it to him, he made known part of it and ignored a part. And when he informed her about it, she said, "Who told you this?" He said, "I was informed by the Knowing, the Acquainted."4. If you two [wives] repent to Allah ﷻ , [it is best], for your hearts have deviated. But if you cooperate against him—then indeed Allah ﷻ ﷻ is his protector, and Gabriel and the righteous of the believers and the angels, moreover, are [his] assistants. 5. Perhaps his Lord, if he divorced you [all], would substitute for him wives better than you—submitting [to Allah ﷻ], believing, devoutly obedient, repentant, worshipping, and traveling—[ones] previously married and virgins.

In this case, Rasulullah ﷺ took the disturbance of this case on himself ﷺ, and preferred seclusion instead of moving on and investigating the case [7]. Similar to Yusuf as, there was the possible case of group collaboration of the women against a person. In the case of Rasulullah ﷺ, this is mentioned with وَإِن تَظَاهَرَا عَلَيْهِ. Today's English terminology uses 'gang up on someone' in popular language. Yet, we need to be careful in the case of Rasulullah ﷺ due to our adab.

Rasulullah ﷺ has taken this disturbance on himself personally in order not to break anyone's heart as mentioned[166] يَا أَيُّهَا النَّبِيُّ لِمَ تُحَرِّمُ مَا أَحَلَّ اللَّهُ لَكَ تَبْتَغِي مَرْضَاتَ أَزْوَاجِكَ وَاللَّهُ غَفُورٌ رَّحِيمٌ {التحريم/1}. This is again a sign of the very high character of Rasulullah ﷺ and there is an implied praise in the expression يَا أَيُّهَا النَّبِيُّ لِمَ تُحَرِّمُ مَا أَحَلَّ اللَّهُ لَكَ تَبْتَغِي مَرْضَاتَ أَزْوَاجِكَ.

Yet, Rasulullah ﷺ had the full tawakkul, taslìm, and tawfidh to Allah ﷻ. Allah ﷻ shows the result of this highest maqãm as[167] وَاللَّهُ مَوْلَاكُمْ وَهُوَ الْعَلِيمُ الْحَكِيمُ {التحريم/2}.

فَإِنَّ اللَّهَ هُوَ مَوْلَاهُ وَجِبْرِيلُ وَصَالِحُ الْمُؤْمِنِينَ وَالْمَلَائِكَةُ بَعْدَ ذَٰلِكَ ظَهِيرٌ {التحريم/4}

عَسَىٰ رَبُّهُ إِن طَلَّقَكُنَّ أَن يُبْدِلَهُ أَزْوَاجًا خَيْرًا مِّنكُنَّ مُسْلِمَاتٍ مُّؤْمِنَاتٍ قَانِتَاتٍ تَائِبَاتٍ عَابِدَاتٍ سَائِحَاتٍ ثَيِّبَاتٍ وَأَبْكَارًا {التحريم/5}

One can see and witness that the cases of the problems related to spousal relationships can deeply affect a person. The quantity and quality of the disturbances and effects can change depending on the individual, gender, and culture.

For example, there can be the case of a husband or a wife who has the full taslim, tawakkul, and tawfidh to Allah ﷻ. The spouse still wants to maintain the relationship of marriage in order to minimize the conflicts although he or she is right and may be 'oppressed' in our modern terms of social work.

In the above ayah, the critical expressions تَبْتَغِي مَرْضَاتَ أَزْوَاجِكَ can indicate the high status of Rasulullah ﷺ in his struggle ﷺ to maintain a

---

166. O Prophet, why do you prohibit [yourself from] what Allah ﷻ has made lawful for you, seeking the approval of your wives? And Allah ﷻ is Forgiving and Merciful.

167. 2. And Allah ﷻ is your protector, and He is the Knowing, the Wise. 4. then indeed Allah ﷻ is his protector, and Gabriel and the righteous of the believers and the angels, moreover, are [his] assistants. 5. Perhaps his Lord, if he divorced you [all], would substitute for him wives better than you—submitting [to Allah] ﷻ , believing, devoutly obedient, repentant, worshipping, and traveling—[ones] previously married and virgins.

positive relationship with everyone, to please them, and not break their hearts.

Similarly, in the same sûrah, Allah ﷻ mentions two cases as[168] ضَرَبَ اللَّهُ مَثَلًا لِّلَّذِينَ كَفَرُوا امْرَأَةَ نُوحٍ وَامْرَأَةَ لُوطٍ كَانَتَا تَحْتَ عَبْدَيْنِ مِنْ عِبَادِنَا صَالِحَيْنِ فَخَانَتَاهُمَا فَلَمْ يُغْنِيَا عَنْهُمَا مِنَ اللَّهِ شَيْئًا وَقِيلَ ادْخُلَا النَّارَ مَعَ الدَّاخِلِينَ. {التحريم/10}

In these cases, again, there are the examples of two husbands, Nuh as and Lut as as the prophets of Allah ﷻ, trying to minimize conflicts to maintain the relationships in their family with full tawakkul, tawfidh, and taslim to Allah ﷻ. Yet, at the same time, these anbiyã, the prophets of Allah ﷻ are dealing with another huge disturbance due to the problems in their qawm, society.

In this case, the wives have the problem of ingratitude and lack of appreciation to Allah ﷻ, generating problems in their relationships with their appreciative and sincere husbands as mentioned ضَرَبَ اللَّهُ مَثَلًا لِّلَّذِينَ كَفَرُوا امْرَأَةَ نُوحٍ وَامْرَأَةَ لُوطٍ كَانَتَا تَحْتَ عَبْدَيْنِ مِنْ عِبَادِنَا صَالِحَيْنِ. Yet, they betrayed them فَخَانَتَاهُمَا.

The women really should ponder in these ayahs their primary relationship with Allah ﷻ and accordingly with their husband as the words فَخَانَتَاهُمَا can indicate. If this primary disposition is missing, then other virtuous deeds can vanish and may not have much value as mentioned in this ayah فَلَمْ يُغْنِيَا عَنْهُمَا مِنَ اللَّهِ شَيْئًا or in the previous ayah as[169] وَإِن تَظَاهَرَا عَلَيْهِ فَإِنَّ اللَّهَ هُوَ مَوْلَاهُ وَجِبْرِيلُ وَصَالِحُ الْمُؤْمِنِينَ وَالْمَلَائِكَةُ بَعْدَ ذَٰلِكَ ظَهِيرٌ {التحريم/4}.

In the case of problems of the man towards women, two cases are also mentioned as[170] وَضَرَبَ اللَّهُ مَثَلاً لِّلَّذِينَ آمَنُوا امْرَأَةَ فِرْعَوْنَ إِذْ قَالَتْ رَبِّ ابْنِ لِي عِندَكَ بَيْتًا فِي الْجَنَّةِ وَنَجِّنِي مِن فِرْعَوْنَ وَعَمَلِهِ وَنَجِّنِي مِنَ الْقَوْمِ الظَّالِمِينَ {التحريم/11} وَمَرْيَمَ ابْنَتَ عِمْرَانَ الَّتِي أَحْصَنَتْ فَرْجَهَا فَنَفَخْنَا فِيهِ مِن رُّوحِنَا وَصَدَّقَتْ بِكَلِمَاتِ رَبِّهَا وَكُتُبِهِ وَكَانَتْ مِنَ الْقَانِتِينَ. {التحريم/12}

---

168. Allah ﷻ presents an example of those who disbelieved: the wife of Noah and the wife of Lot. They were under two of Our righteous servants but betrayed them, so those prophets did not avail them from Allah ﷻ at all, and it was said, "Enter the Fire with those who enter."

169. But if you cooperate against him—then indeed Allah ﷻ is his protector, and Gabriel and the righteous of the believers and the angels, moreover, are [his] assistants.

170. 11. And Allah ﷻ presents an example of those who believed: the wife of Pharaoh, when she said, "My Lord, build for me near You a house in Paradise and save me from Pharaoh and his deeds and save me from the wrongdoing people." 12. And [the example of] Mary, the daughter of 'Imran, who guarded her chastity, so We blew into [her garment] through Our angel, and she believed in the words of her Lord and His scriptures and was of the devoutly obedient.

One can analyze in the above ayahs one of the common problems that man has towards women is oppression. The primary example of this oppression is the case of Fir'awn towards his wife and women as mentioned {التحريم/11} وَنَجِّنِي مِن فِرْعَوْنَ وَعَمَلِهِ وَنَجِّنِي مِنَ الْقَوْمِ الظَّالِمِينَ.

In the case of oppression of women by men, there are individual oppressions of women especially in husband and wife relationships. Also, there is the social oppression of women in the society by generally oppressive rules and policies.

One can remember in the Qurãn different ayahs about the practices of the Fir'awn towards women[171] إِنَّ فِرْعَوْنَ عَلاَ فِي الأَرْضِ وَجَعَلَ أَهْلَهَا شِيَعًا يَسْتَضْعِفُ طَائِفَةً مِّنْهُمْ يُذَبِّحُ أَبْنَاءهُمْ وَيَسْتَحْيِي نِسَاءهُمْ إِنَّهُ كَانَ مِنَ الْمُفْسِدِينَ {القصص/4}.

Another case or example of societal oppression towards women is the example of Maryam as mentioned in the Quran. In this case, she was oppressed in her society and cast away with devastating blame. Allah ﷻ protected and clarified all of this blame and the societal oppression towards her as mentioned[172] وَمَرْيَمَ ابْنَتَ عِمْرَانَ الَّتِي أَحْصَنَتْ فَرْجَهَا فَنَفَخْنَا فِيهِ مِن رُّوحِنَا وَصَدَّقَتْ بِكَلِمَاتِ رَبِّهَا وهِ وَكَانَتْ مِنَ الْقَانِتِينَ {التحريم/12}.

We now return to our original discussion of how one's position can be when facing blame. One can remember the case of Abu Bakr ra as the example of a person being blamed for something who did not defend himself and an angel defended him [19] (hadith# 9411). Rasulullah ﷺ was so pleased with this high stance of Abu Bakr (ra) that he ﷺ was observing the situation and smiling to express this pleasure for this high maqãm of Abu Bakr (ra) until he started defending himself.

Another example is the case of Osman ra. He did not want to defend himself when the protesters wanted to kill him.

One can review the ayah in this section about Yusuf as. Yusuf as preferred with hikmah the second stance of clarifying the problem. Yet, Yusuf as underlined and emphasized the reality of وَمَا أُبَرِّىءُ نَفْسِي إِنَّ النَّفْسَ لأَمَّارَةٌ بِالسُّوءِ إِلاَّ مَا رَحِمَ رَبِّيَ.

In the case of clarifying yourself and defending yourself, there is always the involvement of the nafs as Yusuf as mentions in إِنَّ النَّفْسَ لأَمَّارَةٌ بِالسُّوءِ. Therefore, one should not try to elevate one's nafs, self or ego in

171. Indeed, Pharaoh exalted himself in the land and made its people into factions, oppressing a sector among them, slaughtering their [newborn] sons and keeping their females alive. Indeed, he was of the corrupters.

172. And [the example of] Mary, the daughter of 'Imran, who guarded her chastity, so We blew into [her garment] through Our angel, and she believed in the words of her Lord and His scriptures and was of the devoutly obedient.

the dispositions or discussions of defending oneself as mentioned وَمَا أُبَرِّىءُ نَفْسِي.

The reason is that when one is clarifying oneself, there is always the possibility of arrogance and 'I am better than you' implications. Although the stance of clarifying and defending oneself is normal and acceptable, it can be dangerous and misleading if the person does not maintain balance.

May Allah ﷻ protect us from elevating our nafs, blaming others, talking about others, making giybah of others, being unappreciative of our spouse, oppressing others and our spouse and May Allah[173] ﷻ فَاطِرَ السَّمَاوَاتِ وَالأَرْضِ أَنتَ وَلِيِّي فِي الدُّنُيَا وَالآخِرَةِ تَوَفَّنِي مُسْلِمًا وَأَلْحِقْنِي بِالصَّالِحِينَ {يوسف/101}.

Juz 17

Sûrah 21 – al-Anbiyã

[94][174]

فَمَن يَعْمَلْ مِنَ الصَّالِحَاتِ وَهُوَ مُؤْمِنٌ فَلَا كُفْرَانَ لِسَعْيِهِ وَإِنَّا لَهُ كَاتِبُونَ {الأنبياء/94}

It is interesting to note that the word kufr as كُفْرَانَ is used. This word here is especially used as the opposite of appreciation. In other words, it is emphasized that Allah ﷻ as al-Shakûr appreciates all good efforts of a believer to please Allah ﷻ. This is mentioned as فَمَن يَعْمَلْ مِنَ الصَّالِحَاتِ وَهُوَ مُؤْمِنٌ.

In the literal meaning of kãfir, there is the lack of appreciation and ingratitude. In this regard, kãfir is the one who does not appreciate Allah ﷻ. This appreciation is called tawhid or iman. If this primary, fundamental, and main appreciation is absent, then all others have no foundation to be built upon.

In this perspective, Allah ﷻ teaches us this required primary attitude, quality, and disposition of appreciation as فَلَا كُفْرَانَ لِسَعْيِهِ. All of these efforts are appreciated by Allah ﷻ.

---

173. My Lord, You have given me [something] of sovereignty and taught me of the interpretation of dreams. Creator of the heavens and earth, You are my protector in this world and in the Hereafter. Cause me to die a Muslim and join me with the righteous."

174. So whoever does righteous deeds while he is a believer—no denial will there be for his effort, and indeed We, of it, are recorders.

In addition, the expression وَإِنَّا لَهُ كَاتِبُونَ gives more assurance to the person with ta'kid that the person's good efforts are not evaporated or lost but rather are recorded fully.

It is the meaning of the salah or 'ibadah that the person realizes and embodies their a'jz, and faqr, spiritual and physical poverty in front of Allah ﷻ. Then this person rushes to make sajdah to Rabbul A'lamin with astonishment, awe, and love.

Juz 19

Sûrah 25 al-Furqãn

[63][175]

وَعِبَادُ الرَّحْمَنِ الَّذِينَ يَمْشُونَ عَلَى الْأَرْضِ هَوْنًا وَإِذَا خَاطَبَهُمُ الْجَاهِلُونَ قَالُوا سَلَامًا
{الفرقان/63}

We are in the constant struggles of life. The struggles of life can stem from human relations, finances, deaths, and health. The struggles related with finances and health may not be controlled by the person most of the time and they require active patience with salah and dua to Allah ﷻ for the ease. Yet, the struggles, stresses, or anxieties related with human relations can be somehow manageable when the person focuses on oneself and his or her relation with Allah ﷻ.

The struggles induced by human relations either in the family, social, or professional life can increase or decrease depending on how the person handles them.

One of the ways to decrease the stress, anxiety, grief, anger, and sadness due to human relations is to ignore the engagements of people who are the source of the problem. In this regard, the Qurãn instructs وَإِذَا خَاطَبَهُمُ الْجَاهِلُونَ قَالُوا سَلَامًا.

Sometimes, defending yourself in a blamed position can make you more angry when the person doesn't seem to have any empathy for you and doesn't understand what you are saying. In these situations, maybe in all, the safest way can be to say "peace" with the words or embody this attitude against the rude attitudes of others who don't have empathy.

175. And the servants of the Most Merciful are those who walk upon the earth easily, and when the ignorant address them [harshly], they say [words of] peace,

Juz 21

Sûrah 30-al-Rûm

[17-18][176]

فَسُبْحَانَ اللَّهِ حِينَ تُمْسُونَ وَحِينَ تُصْبِحُونَ {الروم/17} وَلَهُ الْحَمْدُ فِي السَّمَاوَاتِ
وَالْأَرْضِ وَعَشِيًّا وَحِينَ تُظْهِرُونَ {الروم/18}

The essence of the salãh is SubhanAllah, Alhamdulillah, and Allahu Akbar. To emphasize this essential point, there is the dhikr of these phrases thirty-three times after each salah as mentioned by Rasulullah 5] ﷺ].

'Ibadah is the realization of one's own mistakes, faults, slips, and gaffes in front of Rabbul Alamìn, Allah ﷻ. 'Ibadah is the form of turning to Allah ﷻ. In its technical term, one can also call this turning tawbah, inabah, or awbah.

In this sense, there is no distinction between the mistakes, transgressions, faults, slips, or sins that one committed in one's relations with people or Allah ﷻ. In all of the transgressions, the first requirement is to turn to Allah ﷻ.

This turning is called 'ibadah in its general form as salah, ruku, sajdah. In its specific forms this turning can be called tawbah, inabah, and awbah.

We are constantly in the state of hurting others and severing our relationship with Allah ﷻ and all of this leads to hurting ourselves. When we hurt ourselves, we become depressed and sad. How do we become happy and peaceful again?

Allah ﷻ gave us the leave way or resetting these depressive destructive ways of oppressing our own selves. This leave way is the 'ibadah.

A sound person of heart and mind will destroy himself or herself if there is no 'ibadah. He or she would be in the negative states of self-blame leading to depression, regret, and pessimism.

'Ibadah uses these moments of self-accountability and reflection of blame and regret and transforms them into the positive states of reliance on Allah ﷻ . This reliance is based on one's own weakness and

176. 17. So exalted is Allah ﷻ when you reach the evening and when you reach the morning. 18. And to Him is [due all] praise throughout the heavens and the earth. And [exalted is He] at night and when you are at noon.

not dependability on one's own self, but being constantly dependent on Allah ﷻ by asking constant help, seeking refuge, protection, and guidance from Allah ﷻ.

When the person falls into sajdah as mentioned[177] قَالَ لَقَدْ ظَلَمَكَ بِسُؤَالِ نَعْجَتِكَ إِلَى نِعَاجِهِ وَإِنَّ كَثِيرًا مِّنْ الْخُلَطَاء لَيَبْغِي بَعْضُهُمْ عَلَى بَعْضٍ إِلَّا الَّذِينَ آمَنُوا وَعَمِلُوا الصَّالِحَاتِ وَقَلِيلٌ مَّا هُمْ وَظَنَّ دَاوُودُ أَنَّمَا فَتَنَّاهُ فَاسْتَغْفَرَ رَبَّهُ وَخَرَّ رَاكِعًا وَأَنَابَ (سجدة مستحبة) {ص/24}, then these moments open another dimension for the person in his or her spiritual path with Allah ﷻ. The One Who has control of everything can change the hearts of others towards this person. Therefore, one should always maintain the primary concern of turning to Allah ﷻ. This turning is actualized and practically implemented by 'ibadah.

SubhanAllah

True Rububiyyah of Allah ﷻ requires two perspectives and embodiments from the person as the 'abd of Allah ﷻ.

First is that the Authority (Mulk-al-Mālik) of Rububiyyah of Allah ﷻ requires submission and 'ibadah to Allah ﷻ. When a person is under the care of someone, the caretaker tries his or her best to take care of this person. The caretaker does not expect any return or payment for his or her caretaking. With all of his or her effort, if the one who is under this caretaker becomes constantly rude, opposes, and rejects, then the position of the person under care is really not acceptable. The person really needs the caretaker for survival. Yet, there is a rude, belligerent, and ungrateful attitude. Therefore, a sound and logical person really appreciates the caretaker who constantly takes care of him or her and follows his or her instructions. One can see this relationship between a person and his or her parents. At an absolute level, this relationship is between the person and Allah ﷻ.

Second is the Sanctity, Purity, and Holiness (Qudsiyyah-al-Quddûs)) of Rububiyyah of Allah ﷻ . This requires knowing and embodying the Perfectness of Allah ﷻ. If there is any type of human negative thoughts and feelings related with the Qudsiyyah of Allah ﷻ, then this should

177. [David] said, "He has certainly wronged you in demanding your ewe [in addition] to his ewes. And indeed, many associates oppress one another, except for those who believe and do righteous deeds—and few are they." And David became certain that We had tried him, and he asked forgiveness of his Lord and fell down bowing [in prostration] and turned in repentance [to Allah ﷻ].

be removed with istigfar, asking forgiveness from Allah ﷻ and tanzìh, negation of these human renderings for Rabbul Alamìn. In our human realms of following others either as our teachers, parents, or even friends, if we know and think they have some problematic and negative traits or attributes, then we may tend to not follow them.

In reality, Allah ﷻ is the Absolute Perfect as al-Quddus regardless of the people's self-constructed delusional and false renderings. Our relationship with Allah ﷻ requires constant negation of these false and wrong thoughts and feelings from our hearts and minds about Allah ﷻ, the Absolute Perfect, Absolute Pure, al-Quddus with all the Divine Attributes and Names.

Allah ﷻ gives us the opportunity of correcting ourselves with the dhikr of SubhanAllah.

SubhanAllah is the essence of the prayer, dua and one's true connection with Allah ﷻ.

Ma Sabbahnaka Haqqa TasbihaKa Ya Allah! ما سبّحناك حقّ تسبيحك يا الله

AllahuAkbar

The Absolute Power (Qudrah) of Rububiyyah necessitates the person, a'bd or the servant recognizes his or her impotence, fault, weakness, fragility, limitation, poverty, and incapability.

Recognizing one's impotence requires that Allah ﷻ has the Full and Absolute Qudrah.

Recognizing one's fault requires asking forgiveness and turning to the One Who has the ability to forgive.

Recognizing one's weakness requires taking shelter unto the One Who has the ability to protect.

Recognizing one's fragility requires not asking or expecting anything from anyone capable of breaking one's heart at any time, but expecting from the One Who is al-Shakur, appreciates fully and truly all the efforts regardless of their outcome.

Recognizing one's limitation requires seeking for the One, Who does not have any limits.

Recognizing one's poverty requires asking help from the One, Who has the Real Ownership of all Dominions.

Recognizing one's incapability requires finding and seeking encouragement of hope in this life and in the afterlife from the One

Who is Al-Baki, Al-Akhir, Al-Awwal, Al-Hannan, Al-Mannan, and Al-Latìf.

All of the above requires the One Who is Al-Ahad, the One and the Unique.

All of the above requires the One Who is Al-Samad, Independent but not dependent.

All of the above requires the One Who is not like humans, not like creation, not dependent on parents and not having any offspring.

All of the above requires the One Who does not have any equivalence, Who is Allah ﷻ.

With all of the above, one internally and externally cries with ALLAHU AKBAR.

Allahumma Tahir Qulubuna Min Al-kibir, Amìn! اللهم طهر قلوبنا من الكبر ، آمين

Alhamdulillah

The person has constant needs. Realizing these needs is a virtue. Realization of weakness, inability, or powerlessness can all be potentials to cause the person to jump to the next level.

After turning to Allah ﷻ with full physical and spiritual poverty, full absence of physical and spiritual strength, and with full nothingness is the next level up of a higher virtue. At this level, the person can beg, cry, and make dua to Allah ﷻ verbally, immersed in the feelings and emotions of embodiment of this state of faqr and a'jz. This is a state in which the person really acknowledges that he or she cannot live, move, or take a single breath without Allah ﷻ. If Allah ﷻ turns away from this person even less than a second, the person knows, experiences, and fears that he or she is doomed in the endless layers of darkness, loss, pessimism, hopelessness, anxiety, and depression all leading to kufr. In this state, the person begs, cries, and cries to Allah ﷻ that Allah ﷻ does not turn the Divine Fadl and Rahmah away even less than a second from this person. This stage has a very critical stance that the person should constantly remind himself or herself about his or her reality and discharge himself or herself in front of Rabbul A'lamin with crying.

The last and the real stage of this journey regardless of the person's state is always being in gratitude, humility, thankfulness, and appreciation with Rabbul Alamin. This is called the state of hamd. Alhamdulillah is the verbal embodiment of this state. Regardless of the condition of the person, the person realizes, knows, and appreciates existence, imãn, health, food, breathing, seeing, and everything else. If there is any other special bounty that the person is experiencing, the person first needs to think about that in order to realize it and not cover it. Covering the ni'mahs, bounties is kufr. Covering the n'imahs and not thanking Allah ﷻ is disbelief. Therefore, Alhamdulillah is the lifeguard of the person from spiritual death due to kufr. Alhamdulillah is the source of saving oneself from stinginess, misery, pessimism, hopelessness, and anxiety. Alhamdulillah is the source of experiencing more bounty as mentioned by Allah[178] {إبراهيم/7} وَإِذْ تَأَذَّنَ رَبُّكُمْ لَئِن شَكَرْتُمْ لَأَزِيدَنَّكُمْ وَلَئِن كَفَرْتُمْ إِنَّ عَذَابِي لَشَدِيدٌ :ﷻ.

Alhamdulillah,

Alhamdulillah,

Alhamdullilah mil assamawati mil al arda wa [4],

Allahumma Tahir Qulubuna bi Hamdika, Bihaqiqati Alhamdulillah, Amìn.

Allahumma a'inna ala dhikrika wa shukruka wa husnu I'badatika, Amìn!

Juz 27

Sûrah 57 – al-Hadìd

[1][179]

سَبَّحَ لِلَّهِ مَا فِي السَّمَاوَاتِ وَالْأَرْضِ وَهُوَ الْعَزِيزُ الْحَكِيمُ {الحديد/1}

The Passcode and the Perspective

When we analyze and review the perspectives of imãn, we sometimes tend to carry u'lfah, a negative habitual remnant. U'lfah is a problem of habits, when something becomes routine and we don't really remember our initial intention anymore. We take it for granted. We don't appreciate it so that we can increase our benefit from it.

---

178. And [remember] when your Lord proclaimed, 'If you are grateful, I will surely increase you [in favor]; but if you deny, indeed, My punishment is severe.'"

179. Whatever is in the heavens and earth exalts Allah ﷻ, and He is the Exalted in Might, the Wise.

The problem of u'lfah can also happen often with different branches and faculties of imãn.

One of these problems of u'lfah related with one's imãn is related with the phrase and critical expression سَبَّحَ لِلَّهِ. Especially, the critical statement repeatedly appears in the Qurãn as سَبَّحَ لِلَّهِ مَا فِي السَّمَاوَاتِ وَالْأَرْضِ.

Sometimes, it is good to think about and analyze everything for exploration from its opposite perspective, especially in order to break the blockages of u'lfah. In this sense, if one assumes a case or a life without سَبَّحَ لِلَّهِ مَا فِي السَّمَاوَاتِ وَالْأَرْضِ, then what can be the outcome? The outcome is called kufr in its technical term.

The outcome then is certainly very horrifying, depressive, chaotic, anarchic, and alarming. Why?

When a person knows that everything has a purpose, meaning, and goal in a structure under the authority, control, and maintenance of Rabbul Alamìn, then this knowledge and realization in itself removes all of the above negative pessimistic states. This perspective definitely puts the person in ease, comfort, tranquility, calmness, and happiness. This perspective is called imãn in its technical term.

The assumptions and terrifying incidents broadcasted and instilled in people's minds and hearts without imãn undeniably break the spiritual stamina of the person. They block the true purpose, goal, and meaning of a person in life. They remove the hope and encouragement of a person to live and exist in life.

How can a parent with this mindset and perspective soothe his or her five-year-old daughter or son who is horrified by a pandemic virus? How can this parent soothe this child about mass killings happening in the world? How can this parent soothe this child about the loss of a loved one in the family?

This is impossible without the pearl and diamond realities of imãn. With imãn, the person knows with certainty that all of the evil-looking incidents are under the control and service of Allah ﷻ. They are only the simple means and externalities as mentioned in Sûrah Kahf in the story of Musa as with Khidr as.

At a very practical level, if a person sees an animal while walking, he or she may get scared and get extremely uncomfortable if he or she doesn't recognize the animal to be the creation of Allah ﷻ. It has a common purpose and goal like this person. Both this animal and this person work in the same institution for the same goal and purpose. If the person takes refuge in Allah ﷻ, then this animal becomes his or her servant instead of his enemy. There are many examples of this in Islamic history- how even the most wildly defined animals such as tigers or lions can be the servants of people of Allah ﷻ.

One should really imagine the early times of Islam with sahabah Radiyallahu anhum. Whereas before Islam, everything looked scary, intimidating, and dark, after Islam, sahabah Radiyallahu anhum realized the true meanings in their relationship with their purpose and meaning as created by Allah ﷻ. With the presence of Rasulullah ﷺ, the Full Guidance for all, they did have the ability to clearly contrast light and darkness while remembering their past mindsets before Islãm. Therefore, they fully appreciated their new life with imãn.

On the other hand, our Muslim generations inheriting the religion from their parents do not often have this ability to clearly contrast light and darkness. Especially, when there are increased means of distractions in life making it difficult for us to focus, the blurring can be more dramatic between the lights of imãn and darkness of kufr. Unless a catastrophic incident happens in one's life, the person does not fully or truly turn to Allah ﷻ with ikhlas. We think that we are Muslims and we have imãn, yet, we could be far from its essence.

Before it is too late, we should reset ourselves in our goal and intention for our lives. It is very important to go to simple-looking questions such as: what is my goal in this life? How am I spending my short life? This may also be called self-accountability. Yet, it is needed in order to maintain our balance, siratul mustaqim on the path of Allah ﷻ with the guidance of Rasulullah ﷺ.

Taking refuge in Allah ﷻ is remembering and uttering the code of this institutional belonging. Bismillah is the common code and password reminded to the person in every sûrah of the Qurãn. The addition of Ar-Rahman and Ar- Rahìm to this code and password reminds the person that this institution is not an oppressive and abusive one with authority, rules, and slavery.

Yet, it is an institution of mercy, caring, love, kindness, forgiveness, compassion, sympathy, generosity, support, empathy, bounty, amnesty, liberality, tolerance, freedom, affection, warmth, and gentleness.

The person carrying this full passcode of Bismillahi Rahmani Rahim can have the administrator passcode to everything in the universe.

Allahumma J'alna minhum, Amìn. اللهم جعلنا منهم

Juz 28

Sûrah 64 – al-Tagãbun[180]

يَا أَيُّهَا الَّذِينَ آمَنُوا إِنَّ مِنْ أَزْوَاجِكُمْ وَأَوْلَادِكُمْ عَدُوًّا لَّكُمْ فَاحْذَرُوهُمْ وَإِن تَعْفُوا وَتَصْفَحُوا وَتَغْفِرُوا فَإِنَّ اللَّهَ غَفُورٌ رَّحِيمٌ {التغابن/14} إِنَّمَا أَمْوَالُكُمْ وَأَوْلَادُكُمْ فِتْنَةٌ وَاللَّهُ عِندَهُ أَجْرٌ عَظِيمٌ {التغابن/15}

If we analyze the above verse around the word عَدُوًّا, some interesting istinbãt, derivations can be possible.

The same word is used against Jibril as[181] قُلْ مَن كَانَ عَدُوًّا لِّجِبْرِيلَ فَإِنَّهُ نَزَّلَهُ عَلَى قَلْبِكَ بِإِذْنِ اللَّهِ مُصَدِّقاً لِّمَا بَيْنَ يَدَيْهِ وَهُدًى وَبُشْرَى لِلْمُؤْمِنِينَ {البقرة/97} مَن كَانَ عَدُوًّا لِّلَّهِ وَمَلآئِكَتِهِ وَرُسُلِهِ وَجِبْرِيلَ وَمِيكَالَ فَإِنَّ اللَّهَ عَدُوٌّ لِّلْكَافِرِينَ {البقرة/98}.

One can realize that even some people feel animosity and hatred towards the angels who represent goodness, purity, and nobility. For the case of Jibril as, there are narrations of sabab-nuzûl in which some of the ahlu-kitãb, such as the Jews were putting blame on Jibril as, astagfirullah, in the engagements of revelation, astagfirullah. On the other hand, Christians were mixing the role of Jibril as in the encounters of our reality and giving a separate position of Holy Spirit (Ruhul Qudus) in their falsely and wrongly constructed concepts of trinity. One is one extreme and the other is another extreme referred to as ifrãd and tafrìd.

When we analyze the other parts of the Qurãn around the word عَدُوًّا, there may be a common theme that can emerge with a shared meaning of this word. A common theme of this word عَدُوًّا can be anything that hinders the person from reaching his or her goal. This can be any goal. For a kãfir, this goal is to engage in a life to displease Allah ﷻ. This is mentioned as[182] فَالْتَقَطَهُ آلُ فِرْعَوْنَ لِيَكُونَ لَهُمْ عَدُوًّا وَحَزَنًا إِنَّ فِرْعَوْنَ وَهَامَانَ وَجُنُودَهُمَا

180. 14. O you who have believed, indeed, among your wives and your children are enemies to you, so beware of them. But if you pardon and overlook and forgive—then indeed, Allah ﷻ is Forgiving and Merciful. 15. Your wealth and your children are but a trial, and Allah ﷻ has with Him a great reward.

181. 97.Say, "Whoever is an enemy to Gabriel—it is [none but] he who has brought the Qur'an down upon your heart, [O Muhammad ﷺ], by permission of Allah ﷻ, confirming that which was before it and as guidance and good tidings for the believers."98. Whoever is an enemy to Allah and His angels and His messengers and Gabriel and Michael—then indeed, Allah ﷻ is an enemy to the disbelievers.

182. And the family of Pharaoh picked him up [out of the river] so that he would become to them an enemy and a [cause of] grief. Indeed, Pharaoh and Haman and their soldiers were deliberate sinners.

{القصص/8} كَانُوا خَاطِئِينَ. Musa as becomes the عَدُوًّا of Fir'awn because Musa as hinders Fira'wn from reaching his goal of being in engagements that displease Allah ﷻ.

Yet, for a believer, the goal is to please Allah ﷻ in this life and in the afterlife.

Some of the ayahs including this word عَدُوًّا are as follows:[183]

وَإِذَا ضَرَبْتُمْ فِي الأَرْضِ فَلَيْسَ عَلَيْكُمْ جُنَاحٌ أَن تَقْصُرُواْ مِنَ الصَّلاَةِ إِنْ خِفْتُمْ أَن يَفْتِنَكُمُ الَّذِينَ كَفَرُواْ إِنَّ الْكَافِرِينَ كَانُواْ لَكُمْ عَدُوًّا مُّبِينًا {النساء/101}

With the common theme of this word ,عَدُوًّا the above ayah can indicate that some of the people openly categorized as kāfir can have an open stance to prevent a believer from reaching his or her goals in order to please Allah ﷻas mentioned[184] عَدُوًّا مُّبِينًا

وَكَذَلِكَ جَعَلْنَا لِكُلِّ نِبِيٍّ عَدُوًّا شَيَاطِينَ الإِنسِ وَالْجِنِّ يُوحِي بَعْضُهُمْ إِلَى بَعْضٍ زُخْرُفَ الْقَوْلِ غُرُورًا وَلَوْ شَاء رَبُّكَ مَا فَعَلُوهُ فَذَرْهُمْ وَمَا يَفْتَرُونَ {الأنعام/112}

In its specific case and historically, this open enmity towards a believer was displayed by Shaytān in order to distract and deviate the believers from their real goal and purpose of pleasing Allah ﷻ as mentioned[185] وَقُل لِّعِبَادِي يَقُولُواْ الَّتِي هِيَ أَحْسَنُ إِنَّ الشَّيْطَانَ يَنزَغُ بَيْنَهُمْ إِنَّ الشَّيْطَانَ كَانَ لِلإِنْسَانِ عَدُوًّا مُّبِينًا {الإسراء/53}.

Perhaps the person is not a kāfir, yet he or she can still display the attitudes of عَدُوًّا in their spousal relationships especially as mentioned with the harf-jar مِنْ in يَا أَيُّهَا الَّذِينَ آمَنُوا إِنَّ مِنْ أَزْوَاجِكُمْ وَأَوْلَادِكُمْ عَدُوًّا لَّكُمْ. In this case, this is not عَدُوًّا مُّبِينًا, an open enemy. They carry the traits of enmity to hinder the person from their goal and purpose in life.

In the above ayah, {الأنعام/112} Allah ﷻ mentions that there is a wisdom/hikmah of having . عَدُوًّا This is mentioned with وَلَوْ شَاء رَبُّكَ مَا فَعَلُوهُ. The hikmah is to display the real core essence of a human being in one's lifetime struggle to remove spiritual diseases such as hatred, jealousy, and arrogance, and to embody patience and forgiveness. This is

183. And when you travel throughout the land, there is no blame upon you for shortening the prayer, [especially] if you fear that those who disbelieve may disrupt [or attack] you. Indeed, the disbelievers are ever to you a clear enemy.

184. And thus We have made for every prophet an enemy—devils from mankind and jinn, inspiring to one another decorative speech in delusion. But if your Lord had willed, they would not have done it, so leave them and that which they invent.

185. And tell My servants to say that which is best. Indeed, Satan induces [dissension] among them. Indeed Satan is ever, to mankind, a clear enemy.

also mentioned as[186] وَكَذَٰلِكَ جَعَلْنَا لِكُلِّ نَبِيٍّ عَدُوًّا مِّنَ الْمُجْرِمِينَ in وَقَالَ الرَّسُولُ يَا رَبِّ إِنَّ قَوْمِي اتَّخَذُوا هَٰذَا الْقُرْآنَ مَهْجُورًا {الفرقان/30} وَكَذَٰلِكَ جَعَلْنَا لِكُلِّ نَبِيٍّ عَدُوًّا مِّنَ الْمُجْرِمِينَ وَكَفَىٰ بِرَبِّكَ هَادِيًا وَنَصِيرًا {الفرقان/31}. In the case of this ayah, any person preventing the people from disconnecting from the Qurãn, as the only and true Book of Allah ﷻ today, is also in the specific category of عَدُوًّا, as mentioned وَقَالَ الرَّسُولُ يَا رَبِّ إِنَّ قَوْمِي اتَّخَذُوا هَٰذَا الْقُرْآنَ مَهْجُورًا {الفرقان/30}.

In the repeated cases of this word عَدُوًّا, one can realize a teaching of handling this problem. That is to 'move on', 'forgive', and 'not take it too personality' so that the person is not too bothered. This stance is constantly repeated and advised in the Qurãn as in the expression فَذَرْهُمْ وَمَا يَفْتَرُونَ {الأنعام/112} in[187]

وَكَذَٰلِكَ جَعَلْنَا لِكُلِّ نَبِيٍّ عَدُوًّا شَيَاطِينَ الْإِنسِ وَالْجِنِّ يُوحِي بَعْضُهُمْ إِلَىٰ بَعْضٍ زُخْرُفَ الْقَوْلِ غُرُورًا وَلَوْ شَاءَ رَبُّكَ مَا فَعَلُوهُ فَذَرْهُمْ وَمَا يَفْتَرُونَ {الأنعام/112}

the expression وَإِن تَعْفُوا وَتَصْفَحُوا وَتَغْفِرُوا فَاحْذَرُوهُمْ in[188]

يَا أَيُّهَا الَّذِينَ آمَنُوا إِنَّ مِنْ أَزْوَاجِكُمْ وَأَوْلَادِكُمْ عَدُوًّا لَّكُمْ فَاحْذَرُوهُمْ وَإِن تَعْفُوا وَتَصْفَحُوا وَتَغْفِرُوا فَإِنَّ اللَّهَ غَفُورٌ رَّحِيمٌ {التغابن/14}

In all of these above stances, Allah ﷻ instructs us to recognize the people or agents who are going to work against our goals in life of pleasing Allah .ﷻ The primary agent is Shaytãn as mentioned[189] إِنَّ الشَّيْطَانَ لَكُمْ عَدُوٌّ فَاتَّخِذُوهُ عَدُوًّا إِنَّمَا يَدْعُو حِزْبَهُ لِيَكُونُوا مِنْ أَصْحَابِ السَّعِيرِ {فاطر/6}. Then, there will be other ones such as kãfir or people in our families who hinder us explicitly and implicitly from reaching our goal as believers, Allahu A'lam. الله اعلم

186. 30. And the Messenger has said, "O my Lord, indeed my people have taken this Qur'an as [a thing] abandoned."31. And thus have We made for every prophet an enemy from among the criminals. But sufficient is your Lord as a guide and a helper.

187. And thus We have made for every prophet an enemy—devils from mankind and jinn, inspiring to one another decorative speech in delusion. But if your Lord had willed, they would not have done it, so leave them and that which they invent.

188. O you who have believed, indeed, among your wives and your children are enemies to you, so beware of them. But if you pardon and overlook and forgive—then indeed, Allah ﷻ is Forgiving and Merciful.

189. Indeed, Satan is an enemy to you; so take him as an enemy. He only invites his party to be among the companions of the Blaze.

Juz 29

Sûrah 57 – al-Mulk

[2][190]

الَّذِي خَلَقَ الْمَوْتَ وَالْحَيَاةَ لِيَبْلُوَكُمْ أَيُّكُمْ أَحْسَنُ عَمَلًا وَهُوَ الْعَزِيزُ الْغَفُورُ {الملك/2}

Allah ﷻ created the death as mentioned in the ayah with الَّذِي خَلَقَ الْمَوْتَ. In this sense, both the experience of life and the fear of death are the realities. They exist to reveal the essence of a human being as mentioned with لِيَبْلُوَكُمْ أَيُّكُمْ أَحْسَنُ عَمَلًا.

On the other hand, life is a ni'mah. Death is a ni'mah as well. Life is the bounty and ni'mah is the realization of the existence of one person in our realm of life. Death is the bounty and ni'mah is the realization of the leaving behind of the problems, fears, stresses, and prison of this life of the world.

In this regard, death is a bounty and a blessing. It is not something scary for the awliyaullah, the friends of Allah ﷻ. The friends miss the Beloved ﷻ so much that they want the exam of لِيَبْلُوَكُمْ أَيُّكُمْ أَحْسَنُ عَمَلًا to finish with success with the pleasure of Allah ﷻ. Then, the welcome ceremonies in the qabr, grave, and in the Day of Judgment follow.

SubhanAllah, the brother of sleeping is death. Sleeping is a ni'mah from Allah ﷻ. Similarly, his brother death is a ni'mah too. This is mentioned in[191] اللَّهُ يَتَوَفَّى الْأَنفُسَ حِينَ مَوْتِهَا وَالَّتِي لَمْ تَمُتْ فِي مَنَامِهَا فَيُمْسِكُ الَّتِي قَضَى عَلَيْهَا الْمَوْتَ وَيُرْسِلُ الْأُخْرَى إِلَى أَجَلٍ مُسَمًّى إِنَّ فِي ذَلِكَ لَآيَاتٍ لِقَوْمٍ يَتَفَكَّرُونَ {الزمر/42}

[12-14][192]

إِنَّ الَّذِينَ يَخْشَوْنَ رَبَّهُم بِالْغَيْبِ لَهُم مَّغْفِرَةٌ وَأَجْرٌ كَبِيرٌ {الملك/12}

---

190. [He] who created death and life to test you [as to] which of you is best in deed—and He is the Exalted in Might, the Forgiving -

191. Allah ﷻ takes the souls at the time of their death, and those that do not die [He takes] during their sleep. Then He keeps those for which He has decreed death and releases the others for a specified term. Indeed in that are signs for a people who give thought.

192. 12. Indeed, those who fear their Lord unseen will have forgiveness and great reward. 13. And conceal your speech or publicize it; indeed, He is Knowing of that within the breasts. 14. Does He who created not know, while He is the Subtle, the Acquainted?

وَأَسِرُّوا قَوْلَكُمْ أَوِ اجْهَرُوا بِهِ إِنَّهُ عَلِيمٌ بِذَاتِ الصُّدُورِ {الملك/13} أَلَا يَعْلَمُ مَنْ خَلَقَ وَهُوَ اللَّطِيفُ الْخَبِيرُ {الملك/14}

It is interesting to note the teachings of the ayah أَلَا يَعْلَمُ مَنْ خَلَقَ وَهُوَ اللَّطِيفُ الْخَبِيرُ {الملك/14} within the context of the ayahs preceding and coming after it. Sometimes, we forget that Allah ﷻ is aware of all of the internal, minute details of our thoughts and emotions. Allah ﷻ is aware of all of our private and secluded engagements. As we tend to forget this reality, Allah ﷻ mentions it to us to remind us and to rationalize this in humans' understanding of logic.

Juz 30

Sûrah 108 al-Kawthar

[1-3][193]

إِنَّا أَعْطَيْنَاكَ الْكَوْثَرَ {الكوثر/1} فَصَلِّ لِرَبِّكَ وَانْحَرْ {الكوثر/2} إِنَّ شَانِئَكَ هُوَ الْأَبْتَرُ {الكوثر/3}

When we review the uslûb of the Qurãn about the Azamah, Greatness of Allah ,ﷻ one can realize different expressions such as .إِنَّا أَعْطَيْنَاكَ In other parts of the Qurãn, one can realize more explicit perspectives of the Azamah, Greatness of Allah ﷻ such as:[194]

وَقِيلَ يَا أَرْضُ ابْلَعِي مَاءكِ وَيَا سَمَاء أَقْلِعِي وَغِيضَ الْمَاء وَقُضِيَ الأَمْرُ وَاسْتَوَتْ عَلَى الْجُودِيِّ وَقِيلَ بُعْداً لِّلْقَوْمِ الظَّالِمِينَ {هود/44}

ثُمَّ اسْتَوَى إِلَى السَّمَاء وَهِيَ دُخَانٌ فَقَالَ لَهَا وَلِلْأَرْضِ ائْتِيَا طَوْعًا أَوْ كَرْهًا قَالَتَا أَتَيْنَا طَائِعِينَ {فصلت/11}[195]

If one really reviews the above ayahs, one can clearly say the shãdah as ashadu an La ilaha illa Allah wa ashadu anna Muhammadan abduhu

193. 1. Indeed, We have granted you, [O Muhammad ﷺ], al-Kawthar. 2. So pray to your Lord and sacrifice [to Him alone]. 3. Indeed, your enemy is the one cut off.
194. And it was said, "O earth, swallow your water, and O sky, withhold [your rain]." And the water subsided, and the matter was accomplished, and the ship came to rest on the [mountain of] Judiyy. And it was said, "Away with the wrongdoing people."
195. Then He directed Himself to the heaven while it was smoke and said to it and to the earth, "Come [into being], willingly or by compulsion." They said, "We have come willingly."

wa Rasuluhu because we witness the clear Azamah, Greatness of Allah ﷻ in these verses. If we assume for a second that a person is originating the above statements from within himself or herself, then this person, for sure, will be deemed to be crazy, foolish, or insane in our rational and sound judgment of logic. The Azamah of these above verses requires a Being, Allah ﷻ showing the clear and distinct Greatness of Allah ﷻ. The above verses themselves are sufficient to prove the authenticity of the Qurãn and that the Qurãn is from Rabbul A'lamin, Allah ﷻ.

In the expression of shadah, abduhu clearly indicates that the Qurãn is not the word of Rasulullah ﷺ. The expression Rasuluhu indicates that Rasulullah is delivering the message to humans as ordered by Allah ﷻ. The Azamah of Allah ﷻ requires the tawhid as La ilaha illa Allah as the core of the shãdah.

Allahumma Ja'alna min al-Muwahiddìn, Amìn.

One of the meanings of الْكَوْثَرَ is khayr kathir, a lot of good deeds. When one thinks about the deeds of Rasulullah ﷺ , his ﷺ deeds are endless due to the deeds of the ummah. All of the deeds of the ummah are also credited to the Rasulullah ﷺ due to the initial starting point of this ummah. This ummah with its deeds is the best ummah among all as mentioned[196] كُنتُمْ خَيْرَ أُمَّةٍ أُخْرِجَتْ لِلنَّاسِ تَأْمُرُونَ بِالْمَعْرُوفِ وَتَنْهَوْنَ عَنِ الْمُنكَرِ وَتُؤْمِنُونَ بِاللَّهِ وَلَوْ آمَنَ أَهْلُ الْكِتَابِ لَكَانَ خَيْرًا لَّهُم مِّنْهُمُ الْمُؤْمِنُونَ وَأَكْثَرُهُمُ الْفَاسِقُونَ {آل عمران/104}.

The best ummah with the utmost and highest khayr good deeds as mentioned كُنتُمْ خَيْرَ أُمَّةٍ أُخْرِجَتْ لِلنَّاسِ has the highest Nabiyy and Rasûl who is Rasulullah ﷺ. Therefore, the word الْكَوْثَرَ in إِنَّا أَعْطَيْنَاكَ الْكَوْثَرَ {الكوثر/1} [197]can indicate this highest level of khayr of Rasulullah ﷺ as the sabab of the highest level of khayr in the collective body, referred to as ummah as mentioned in كُنتُمْ خَيْرَ أُمَّةٍ أُخْرِجَتْ لِلنَّاسِ.

In this regard, the word الْكَوْثَرَ khayr kathir, a lot of good deeds, leads Rasulullah ﷺ to the maqãm of Mahmûd as mentioned وَمِنَ اللَّيْلِ فَتَهَجَّدْ بِهِ نَافِلَةً لَّكَ عَسَىٰ أَن يَبْعَثَكَ رَبُّكَ مَقَامًا مَّحْمُودًا {الإسراء/79}. The ummah of Rasulullah ﷺ is in constant dua with billions of hands every day raising to Allah ﷻ after each athan asking Allah ﷻ to grant this maqãm for Rasulullah

196. You are the best nation produced [as an example] for mankind. You enjoin what is right and forbid what is wrong and believe in Allah ﷻ . If only the People of the Scripture had believed, it would have been better for them. Among them are believers, but most of them are defiantly disobedient.

197. Indeed, We have granted you, [O Muhammad ﷺ], al-Kawthar.

ﷺ. InshAllah, for sure, Allah ﷻ answers the dua of the ummah for the Habib ﷺ to be in the maqãm of Mahmûd as he ﷺ is also the imam of mutahhajjidûn as mentioned وَمِنَ اللَّيْلِ فَتَهَجَّدْ بِهِ نَافِلَةً لَّكَ عَسَىٰ أَن يَبْعَثَكَ رَبُّكَ مَقَامًا مَّحْمُودًا {الإسراء/79}.

Absence of Barakah & Success without Rasulullah ﷺ

When we review the ayah, إِنَّ شَانِئَكَ هُوَ الْأَبْتَرُ {الكوثر/3}[198] we can realize one of the primary realities about Rasulullah ﷺ, the sunnah, and the hadith of Rasulullah ﷺ. If a person does not love Rasulullah ﷺ and take the teachings of Rasulullah ﷺ as the milestones, then these efforts will not be accepted by Allah ﷻ and they would all be لأَبْتَر.

That is, all of these efforts will be futile, fruitless, vain, pointless, useless, ineffectual, ineffective, inefficacious, to no effect, of no use, in vain, to no avail, unavailing; unsuccessful, failed, thwarted; unproductive, barren, unprofitable, abortive; impotent, hollow, empty, forlorn, idle, hopeless, worthless, and bootless [2].

No one can claim that he or she is on the right path without the love of Rasulullah ﷺ. Absence of love for Rasulullah ﷺ and absence of love and practice of the sunnah of Rasulullah ﷺ can cause all of the efforts to be in vain as mentioned إِنَّ شَانِئَكَ هُوَ الْأَبْتَرُ {الكوثر/3}.

When we analyze إِنَّ شَانِئَكَ, one can realize that there is a qasam, ta'kid and emphasis with إِنَّ to this reality. This reality of the absence of barakah and success in all of the efforts is due to the absence of inclusion of the love and the sunnah, teachings of Rasulullah ﷺ, al-Habìb ﷺ.

Then, the personal pronoun كَ in شَانِئَكَ shows another level of ta'kid and emphasis indicating the high status of Rasulullah ﷺ with Allah ﷻ.

This maqam is in such a high status that no one can truly reach to Allah ﷻ without crossing the path of Rasulullah ﷺ as mentioned in إِنَّ شَانِئَكَ هُوَ الْأَبْتَرُ {الكوثر/3}.

Unfortunately, today and in the past, there were a lot of misfortunate and misguided people claiming to follow the Qurãn and the teachings of Allah ﷻ. Yet, they were trying to differentiate, give less value, or purposefully ignore and devalue the sunnah, teachings of Rasulullah ﷺ implicitly or explicitly. Yet, these people did not realize these clear

198. Indeed, your enemy is the one cut off.

teachings of the Qurān as[199] {الكوثر/3} إِنَّ شَانِئَكَ هُوَ الأَبْتَرُ or[200] إِنَّ الَّذِينَ يَكْفُرُونَ بِاللهِ وَرُسُلِهِ وَيُرِيدُونَ أَن يُفَرِّقُواْ بَيْنَ اللهِ وَرُسُلِهِ وَيقُولُونَ نُؤْمِنُ بِبَعْضٍ وَنَكْفُرُ بِبَعْضٍ وَيُرِيدُونَ أَن يَتَّخِذُواْ بَيْنَ ذَلِكَ سَبِيلاً {النساء/150}

May Allah ﷻ protect us and guide us on the true path of Rasulullah ﷺ, Sahibì Maqãm Mahmûd, Amìn!

199. Indeed, your enemy is the one cut off.

200. Indeed, those who disbelieve in Allah ﷻ and His messengers and wish to discriminate between Allah ﷻ and His messengers and say, "We believe in some and disbelieve in others," and wish to adopt a way in between -

BIBLIOGRAPHY

[1] U. P. Oxford, "Oxford Dictionaries," 2016. [Online]. Available: http://www.oxforddictionaries.com/us/definition/american_english/. [Accessed 2016].

[2] M. Al-Bukhari, The translation of the meanings of Sahih Al-Bukhari, Kazi Publications, 1986.

[3] T. English, " interesting engineering," 07 09 2019. [Online]. Available: www. interestingengineering.com. [Accessed 24 April 2020].

[4] H. Baghawi, Tafsir al-Baghawi al-musamma Maʻalim al-tanzil, Bayrut: Dar al-Maʻrifah, 1987.

[5] A. Muslim, Sahih Muslim (translated by Siddiqui, A.), Peace Vision, 1972.

[6] I. Majah, Sunan Ibn Majah, Darus-Salam, 2007.

[7] I. A. I. A. Al-Wahidi, Alwajizu fi tafsiriil kitabil Aziz, Darul Qalam & Dar Shamia.

[8] S. Abu-Dawud, Sunan Abu Dawud, Riyadh: Darussalam, 2008.

[9] A. i. a.-H. Bayhaqī, 'Shuab -ul- Iman, Bayrūt : Dār al-Kutub al-ʻIlmīyah, 2008.

[10] S. Vahide, The Collection of Light, ihlas nur publication, 2001.

[11] I. A. H. Gazzali, Ihya Ulum ad-din, Fonts Vitae, 2019.

[12] M. Al-Ghazzali, Al-Ghazzali on Knowing Yourself and God, Kazi Publications Inc., 2003.

[13] W. J. Nichols, Blue Mind, Little, Brown, 2014.

[14] P. E. L. Judy T. Tanner, Springs and Bottled Waters of the World Ancient History, Source, Occurrence, Quality and Use, Springer Berlin Heidelberg, 2012.

[15] A. a.-Q. S. Tabarani, Mujam al Kabir, Beirut: DKI, 2007.

[16] M. F. G., Ijaz of the Quran, Nile, 2008.

[17] N. A.-D. A. A.-H. ʻ. I. A. B. Haythami, Majma' al-zawa'id, Turath For Solutions , 2013.

[18] S. Ahmad, Interviewee, *Imam-Masjid As-Salam.* [Interview]. March 2020.

[19] A. B. Hanbal, Musnad Imam Ahmad Ibn Hanbal, Dar-Us-Salam Publications, 2012.

[20] M. Asad, The message of the Quran: Translated and explained., Al-Andalus Gibraltar , 1980.

[21] A. An-Nasa'i, Sunan An-Nasai, Riyadh: Daraussalalm, 2007.

AUTHOR BIO

Dr. Kumek had classical training in Islamic sciences from the respected Shuyûqh/Teachers of Turkey, India, Egypt, Yemen, Somalia, Morocco, Sudan, and the United States. He stayed and studied classical Islamic sciences in Egypt and Turkey as well.

In his Western training, education and teaching experience, Dr. Kumek has acted as the religious studies coordinator at State University of New York (SUNY) Buffalo State and taught undergraduate and graduate courses in religious studies at SUNY at Buffalo State, Niagara University, Daemen College and Harvard Divinity School. Dr. Kumek also pursued doctorate degree in physics at SUNY at Buffalo published academic papers in the areas of quantum physics and medical physics. Then, he decided to engage with the world of social sciences through social anthropology, education, and cultural anthropology in his doctorate studies and subsequently, spent a few years as a research associate in the anthropology department of the same university and subsequently, completed a postdoctoral fellowship at Harvard Divinity school. Some of his book titles include sociology through religion, religious literacy through ethnography, selected passages from the Qurãn, selected passages from the Hadith (titled as Rasulullah ﷺ) and selected prayers of the Prophet Muhammad ﷺ (titled as Pearls and Diamonds). Dr. M. Yunus Kumek is currently teaching on Muslim Ministry and Spiritual Care at Harvard Divinity School.

ACKNOWLEDGMENTS

I would like to thank all my unnamed teachers, friends, and students for their input, ideas, suggestions, help, and support during and before the preparation of this book.

I would like to thank Dr. David Banks, faculty of the Department of Anthropology, State University of New York (SUNY), Sister Toni Hajdaj, Sister Umm Aisha, Dr. AbdulAhad, Br. Ali Rifat and His wife Sister Yildiz at-Turki, Sheikh Dr. Omar of Maryland al-Hindi, Sheikh Tamer of Buffalo, and Sheikh Ali of Hartford Seminary, Sisters Asya Hamad, Amina Osman, and Fatima Samrodia of Darul-Ulum Madania of Buffalo for all their editing, suggestions and comments.

I want to also thank the team of Medina House Publishing in all their preparations and efforts at all stages of this book especially Br. Murat, Br. Khalid (Halit), Br. Mehmet (Matt) and Sister Karen.

Lastly, I would like to thank all of my family members for their patience with me during the preparation of this book.

We ask Allah ﷻ to accept all our efforts with the Divine Karam, Fadl, and Grace but not with our faulty and limited efforts deeming rejection. اللَّهُمَّ صلِّ عَلى سَيِّدِناَ وَ حَبِيْبَنَا وَ مَوْلَانَا مُحَمَّد.

Index

J

K

L

M

P

Q

R

S

T

V

W

www.ingramcontent.com/pod-product-compliance
Lightning Source LLC
LaVergne TN
LVHW051006080826
845145LV00009B/2487

* 9 7 8 1 9 5 0 9 7 9 3 3 2 *